Life to Afterlife – Helping

ISBN: 979848

Copyright © 2021 Elizabeth Boisson

All rights reserved.

Table of Contents

Foreword by Suzanne Giesemann..5
Foreword by Maureen Hancock..13
Introduction by Elizabeth Boisson..17
The Producer, Craig McMahon...21
Our Kids..25
   Morgan James Pierre Boisson & Chelsea.....................................27
   Susan Marie Giesemann-Babich..39
   Tyler John Allen...45
   Carly Elizabeth Hughes..53
   Quinton Stone Jackson..61
   Griffin Clyde Olsen..71
   Austin Jordan Alegre..81
   Derrick Dean Courtney..89
   Garrett Martin Savoie..97
   Sean Patrick McCarthy..105
   Garrett Nathan Ziff..115
   Devon Harper Hollahan...123
   Brandon Blake Donald Ireland..135
   Andy 'Sunshine' Hull...149
   Kyle Aden Erickson...157
The Children of Our Remaining Board Members......................................165
   Bailey Caroline Durham..167
   Wendy Ford & Haley Veronica Ford...171
   Shayna Elayne Smith...177
How to Heal from the Passing of a Child...190
Resources..193
Kiara Kharpertian..195
Gratitude...196
Our Contributors...197

Foreword by Suzanne Giesemann

Chances are, if you're reading this book, someone you dearly love has died. You have a new and insatiable interest in the Afterlife. The contributors to this book, "Life to Afterlife", can identify with this thirst for knowledge about our loved ones' new life. And that's where the paradox becomes apparent: If you believe that death is merely a transition to an alternate form of reality-- that life goes on (and it most certainly does) --then it's not really the AFTERlife!

As the many "No Other Explanation" moments shared throughout this hope-filled book attest to, the body may die, but the eternal aspect of all of us—the soul—continues on in what should more accurately be called "the Everlife."

Each of the stories in this book follows a similar theme. Each springs from an event that we in this Earthly realm would consider a tragedy. And indeed, when someone we love with all our hearts is no longer physically present, the word "tragedy" seems appropriate. Yet thankfully, each of these stories shows that the transition to the next chapter of the soul's eternal journey is not tragic from the soul's point of view. If you gain anything at all from this book, may it be the awareness that out of our greatest challenges comes the greatest growth for our souls.

As the stepmother of Susan Marie Giesemann-Babich, one of the daughters featured in this book, I can relate to the stories shared by my fellow members of Helping Parents Heal (HPH). I also bring to the table my experiences as a former U.S. Navy Commander turned professional medium, as the direct result of Susan's passing. As such, it was a tremendous honor to be asked by producer Craig McMahon to be included in his documentary, *Life to Afterlife: Mom, Can You Hear Me?*

I agreed to fly from my home in South Carolina to Arizona for the filming. Craig asked me to perform a group reading for a special gathering of HPH parents while I was there. The plan was for me to travel with my dear friend and neighbor, Irene Vouvalides, Vice President of HPH. Irene's chapter in this book about her daughter Carly will surely touch your heart.

The day before our flight to Arizona was the anniversary of Carly's transition. I offered to sit with Irene and see what messages Carly had for her mother on this significant date. Always a strong communicator, Carly came through with beautiful validations that in spite of her death, she is still very much a part of her family's life. One thing Carly said, however, left Irene scratching her head: "Have you seen the deer yet?" Carly asked from across the veil.

Irene could not make any connection with deer, so we set the question aside, hoping it would make sense later.

Upon our arrival in Arizona, Irene and I were treated to dinner at the home of Lynn and Jeff Hollahan. We were joined by Elizabeth and Cyril Boisson. It was a joyous reunion for the six of us—minus my husband, Ty, and Irene's husband Tony, who were unable to make the trip. We four couples had been brought together by our children in spirit, a story detailed in my book, *Still Right Here*.

With some excitement, Irene stepped to my side and asked, "Did you see the photo Elizabeth took this morning?" I replied that I had not. Elizabeth took out her phone and showed me a photo of the fourteen deer that had showed up in her driveway that morning. We raised our glasses and celebrated another angelversary "Wow" from Carly.

While enjoying our meal in the Hollahan's dining room, we chatted excitedly about the group reading to be held in that same room the following morning. As Jeff and Lynn discussed rearranging the furniture for the group of twenty parents, I became aware of a presence. I smiled in recognition and announced to the group, "Devon is here."

You will read about Devon, the Hollahan's ever-vibrant son, later in this book. Tonight, he wanted us to know that all the kids of the parents in the group were excited about the next day's get-together.

"Devon says that he and the other kids in spirit will be spending the night here in the dining room," I reported, "and they brought their sleeping bags." He adds, 'It won't be the first time.'"

I tend to hear the messages I deliver from spirit with a skeptic's approach, always asking, *Where's the validation?* Truth be told, as I passed along Devon's message, the former military officer in me felt a bit silly. *All of our kids would be spending the night on the floor in spirit sleeping bags.*

Jeff and Lynn exchanged knowing smiles, and Jeff explained, "In Devon's senior year of college, he showed up one night unexpectedly with twenty members of his University of Arizona Ultimate Frisbee team. They had a match at a nearby field the next day, and they all brought their sleeping bags and crashed on the floor." Devon was right: It wasn't the first time.

The next morning, twenty HPH parents gathered in the Hollahans' dining room. The love in the room was palpable. Each person present chattered excitedly, comfortable to be among kindred spirits and eager to connect with their child. Each wore a nametag that included the name of their child.

Craig checked the lights and cameras and then took a seat in front of the group next to me. I felt the children gathering behind the closed door of the guest room across the hall. As the filming began, a hush fell over the group, and I clearly sensed the children parade into the room and stand behind their respective parents.

Craig had prepared a list of questions about the Afterlife for the children in spirit. I was to be their voice as they answered. It was an unusual situation, for unlike some other mediums, I don't see those in spirit. I feel their personalities, hear their words, and see images they put into my awareness. Happily, I have learned over the years that we don't need to visually observe those who have passed in order for them to validate their presence.

Because this was not a standard gallery reading where spirits simply step forward and provide evidence to the medium, I wasn't sure how the event would go. I needn't have worried. Those in spirit are as clever as they were in their physical incarnation, if not more so. As Craig asked each question, one of the children would enter my awareness with an answer, identifying themselves by means of a specific piece of evidence.

In response to one of Craig's questions, one child showed me a Tonka Toy dump truck. Without hesitation, Ernie and Kristine Jackson raised their hands. "That's Quinton!" they said, referring to the young boy you will meet in Quinton's chapter. Ernie explained: when he and Kristine purchased a home for their daughter and her husband, a yellow Tonka toy appeared in the backyard, a toy that had not been there when they initially walked the property. Seeing it, they knew right away that Quinton had left it.

To this day, that yellow Tonka Toy sits on a shelf in the Jacksons' garage, a keepsake from their son. Clearly, Quinton knew about the truck and was eager to answer Craig's question.

As Craig went down his list, the children demonstrated that they knew in advance what questions he would ask, for several chose to answer questions that were particularly relevant to their personality or background. Mark Ireland's son, Brandon, whom you will get to know in this book, made his presence known that afternoon by showing me an abacus, which reflected his skill at math. Brandon offered to answer the next question on the list. Unbeknownst to anyone in the room except Craig, the next question dealt with science, a subject that Brandon, a senior in high school when he transitioned, had talked about possibly majoring in at college.

As the two-hour session came to an end, Craig asked the final question on his list: "Do any of the kids have an urgent message for someone in the room?"

The image of two people toasting with champagne flashed in my mind's eye, along with the awareness that one of the couples present had an anniversary coming up in the next few days. Kim Courtney raised her hand and identified her son, Derrick, whom you will read about in Kim and Derrick's chapter.

Derrick showed me his mother's swimming pool. The locals laughed. Being an out-of-towner, I was one of the few in the room who was not aware that Kim is a well-respected swimming teacher and coach in the area. She had not just one pool at her house, but two.

Derrick then showed me the frightening scenario of a baby who was in danger of drowning in one of Kim's pools if she wasn't promptly taught how to swim. The child appeared to be about eighteen months old. I emphasized that Derrick meant this outcome was not just a possibility, but a strong probability, if someone did not act swiftly.

Kim's eyes widened. Her granddaughter, who was exactly that age, was currently staying at her house, and Kim had been anxious because the child did not yet know how to swim. As a result of Craig's question and Derrick's urgent message, Kim called home immediately and ensured the baby's safety until they could get her a water proximity bracelet and swimming lessons.

When the session ended, we all rejoiced over the experience of such a special reunion. Only later did we make the connection between the fourteen deer who had appeared at Elizabeth's house the previous day and the fourteen children who had shown up to educate us about the Afterlife.

Awareness of the connectedness of all life led me to research the metaphysical significance of a deer's appearance in one's life. Interestingly, a deer's arrival symbolizes facing challenging situations or having problems achieving peace.

You may be reading this book because you are facing one of the greatest challenges we as humans can be given: accepting and dealing with the transition of a loved one. In this helpful, healing book, you will find you are not alone. The touching, true stories shared here may be emotionally difficult to read yet learning from real-life people like yourself brings another realization: through them, you will be reassured that there is indeed an Everlife after this one, where you will once again join those who have moved on and that life here on Earth is still very much worth living. Knowing this will help you find reasons to smile again and will bring you inestimable peace.

-Evidential Medium Suzanne Giesemann, author of **Messages of Hope** *and* **Still Right Here**

Foreword by Maureen Hancock

How do you survive the physical passing of your child? I remember when my sister Rosie lost her precious 19-year-old son, Sean Michael, in a tragic accident. The police managed to locate me and asked me to accompany them on their difficult mission to inform my sister that her only son was gone. Time stood still for our whole family. As a spirit medium, I was able to perceive that my nephew was smiling and at peace, but as a sister, I joined Rosie as we shrieked, trembled, and collapsed in each other's arms. Then, literally moments after the police had delivered the horrific news, Sean appeared in the window, wearing his signature white tank top, grinning and waving to us! We were immediately blessed with the hope of an Afterlife.

If you have found your way to this book, perhaps you too are on a journey to find your way back to hope. In my role as a medium, I help the grieving create a strong, nonphysical relationship with their loved ones in spirit. Those left behind need to know that not only do their loved ones continue to exist in some form and dimension, but that they still play a role in the lives of their friends and family here on Earth. In recent years a significant shift in belief systems has occurred throughout the globe. Millions are reaching out for answers, struggling to understand death in the face of tragedy and loss. According to the Reverend Andrew M. Greeley, a sociologist at the University of Chicago, 81 percent of Americans believe in an Afterlife. This helps explain the growing interest of Americans in books on the subject matter of life after death.

In "Life to Afterlife," Shining Light Parents share their heartfelt stories about the passing of their children and how they survive and thrive in the wake of the unimaginable. Simple acts like going to the grocery store, running into friends around town, attending graduations, funerals, or birthday parties can be torture for those left behind. These true-life stories explore in-depth mind-blowing signs from beyond! These profound connections from the other side will offer readers strength, understanding, and new beginnings as these parents share how their pain becomes transformed into newfound hope, and a celebration of life both here and beyond.

I had the pleasure of being introduced to this organization, Helping Parents Heal, through Mark Ireland, a Shining Light Dad and co-founder of HPH. It was my honor and pleasure to bring Mark's son, Brandon, through from the higher side. Through Mark, I was introduced to Elizabeth Boisson, President and co-founder, and Irene Vouvalides, Vice President, of HPH. Elizabeth asked me to be part of the documentary by producer Craig McMahon, Life to Afterlife: Mom, Can You Hear Me? This production is a must-watch! Through live Zoom offerings, I've been able to connect many of the Shining Light Parents to their beautiful children. The kids often say to me, "I'm not dead, I'm just different."

This group is like no other I've come across. It offers a unique avenue of relief for the grief that accompanies the loss of a child. As

I say in my book, The Medium Next Door, "The bonds of love cannot be broken by this temporary physical separation."

-Evidential Medium Maureen Hancock, author of **The Medium Next Door**

Introduction by Elizabeth Boisson

It is an immense honor to bring these chapters about our children to you. All of the parents in the book are members of Helping Parents Heal, a nonprofit organization created in 2012 that offers support for parents and families who have experienced the passing of a child. We were honored to have Craig McMahon feature our nonprofit in his documentary, 'Life to Afterlife; Mom, Can You Hear Me?' in 2019.

Craig contacted me at the Afterlife Institute Symposium in September 2018 about interviewing parents who had survived the passing of a child. When we first met, I was concerned about the privacy of the cherished friends who would be part of this documentary. However, after speaking with Craig, I was convinced of his sincerity and compassion. I realized that a documentary that showed that it is genuinely possible to survive the passing of a child would offer significant healing if it became a reality. Finding out that Craig was a Shining Light Sibling sealed the deal.

The parents who participated in the film were grateful for the opportunity to talk about their children and their healing journeys. Other parents need to know that life does not end after their child passes. We can move forward, knowing that our children are still with us.

Soon after listening to Craig's vision of the interviews, I contacted my closest friends who shared this journey with me and lived near the filming location. Many were Board Members of Helping Parents Heal. I spoke to Irene Vouvalides, the Vice President and Conference Director of Helping Parents Heal, about the project and convinced her to fly to Arizona to join us. Irene and I speak multiple times a day, both about HPH and our healing journeys, and I genuinely don't know what I would do without her.

Craig filmed each of the parents using the same set of questions. Most of the answers that made it into the documentary were relatively uncontroversial. However, much of what Craig filmed was pretty remarkable. The parents who participated in the documentary have healed and moved forward after the passing of one or more children, although most believed that it would be impossible to do so. In addition, each parent has experienced a great deal of collateral beauty along the way. Signs from their children that we cannot explain away. Messages of hope that show that they are with us on this healing journey. Nonetheless, to protect and maintain the parents' credibility, Craig decided to keep the footage subdued.

Still, the kids wanted to tell their stories. While I was being interviewed by Jamie and Maggie Clark in July 2021 for their podcast, Psychic Evolution, Jamie surprised me with a message from my son Morgan. He told me that I needed to write a book about Craig's movie and to ask the parents to write a chapter about each of their children. After that, the book came together at lightning speed. Irene Vouvalides asked Zoe Kharpertian, a Shining Light Mom and member of our group, to edit our chapters, and she generously agreed. Zoe realized the magnitude of the job, but she accepted it with grace and style.

I am grateful that through this book, those who have seen Craig's beautiful film will be able to understand how much more there is to the story. We invited our three remaining Board Members to join in. Each of the 19 Shining Light Parents who are a part of the book lives with one foot here on earth and one foot on the other side with our kids. And this journey, which is one that we would wish on no one, has become something rather magical.

As members of Helping Parents Heal, we do not call ourselves 'bereaved,' which is one of the saddest words in the English language. Suzanne Giesemann, who has been an enormous support to Helping Parents Heal, has coined a beautiful term to replace it. We call ourselves Shining Light Parents because we know that the light of our beautiful children shines through us and helps us to heal.

If you have experienced the passing of a child or a sibling, know that you are not alone. We understand your journey, and we walk the same path. Please consider joining us at Helping Parents Heal. Together, we can move forward and grow in spirit.

-Elizabeth Boisson, Shining Light Mom of Morgan and Chelsea, President and Co-Founder, Healing Parents Heal

The Producer: Craig McMahon

As a Documentary filmmaker, my goal in creating 'Life to Afterlife: Mom, Can You Hear Me?' was to bring awareness to the healing that can occur when we are aware that our loved ones on the other side are happy, healthy, and whole. I sat down with seventeen parents who have had a child pass. These parents are from the nonprofit support group "Helping Parents Heal." Like these parents, I am no stranger to loss.

In 1972, when I was just nine years old, my brother Cary passed. He was only eighteen years old and had just gotten married to his new wife, who was pregnant, in Chicago. They set off in a travel trailer and headed to Florida for their honeymoon. When they reached Valdosta, Georgia, Cary fell asleep at the wheel and wrecked the travel trailer. He then attempted to direct traffic around the accident site in the middle of the night and was hit and killed.

Later, when my mom told me that Cary had transitioned, I asked her, 'What does that mean?' She replied that 'We won't see Cary-he's gone.' However, I couldn't grasp or understand this explanation. At the same time, my father, a longtime Catholic, became angry at his religion and God because of Cary. Dad became an atheist.

Cary's passing sent my mom and me in a very different direction spiritually. The two of us started a lifelong conversation about the meaning of death. As a Shining Light Sibling, I watched how my parents dealt with these devastating blows to our family. Mom and Dad divorced soon after. Out of this tragedy, my mother opened a hypnosis institute in Chicago to help others during periods of grief. I grappled with the hole these tragedies left in the hearts of my family members, and I was determined to understand why my family had to go through such pain and hardship.

Later, my oldest brother, Alan, went through bouts of depression. Alan took his life at the age of 43 years after having trouble with the law. He left behind a wife and two children who had just entered high school. Within a few years, both my mom and dad joined my two brothers.

I began to spend time in meditation and realized that nothing else really interested me. However, at age 21, my Spirit Guides told me, 'Why are you so enamored with meditation? You need to get a life!' Therefore, I got married and had a child. Then 30 years later, my spirit team reintroduced themselves and set me on a new journey to create the 'Life to Afterlife' spirituality series and the 'Spirit Box' series. During this time, my psychic ability and knowledge of the Afterlife have improved. Archangel Michael, Buddha, and Jesus are now my friends and protectors. I have realized that I am simply the tool to bring this message to a larger audience.

Most recently, I experienced a significant shift in my life through solitude, which encouraged looking within. I am now in service of the divine to help humanity. I realize the gravity of my responsibilities to help people understand that we don't die and are here to learn. I am blessed to create platforms to demonstrate all the journeys of the exceptional people I meet.

Life to Afterlife: Mom, Can You Hear Me? explores a significant shift in perspective that progresses as a parent develops communication with their child in spirit. In this documentary, seventeen parents start from the beginning of their journeys. They discuss what life was like before, during, and after the passing of their child. They also talk about their perspectives on anger, joy, happiness, guilt, marriage, culture, and religion. The story then arrives at a profound central question: "Where is my child now?" Having an open dialogue about these events sheds light and understanding on several complex and challenging questions and encourages a joyful and purposeful life.

-Craig McMahon, Shining Light Sibling of Cary and Alan and Producer of the 'Life to Afterlife' Spirituality Series

Our Kids

Morgan James Pierre Boisson & Chelsea

On November 23rd, 1988, Morgan was born in Montpellier in the south of France. I first arrived in this historic university town in 1983 as an exchange student from the University of North Carolina at Chapel Hill and returned two years later as a graduate assistant at the Université Paul Valéry. From the moment that I held him in my arms, I felt Morgan's enormous bright light. However, even then I had a feeling deep inside that he would not be here for long. This foreboding caused me constant apprehension throughout his life, further intensified by the fact that I never felt it for my other children.

My husband Cyril had previously lived in Africa for most of his life. His parents were still there, so a few weeks after Morgan's birth, we set off to N'Djamena, Chad, to show off our adorable baby boy. The trip turned into an arduous adventure. Two days into our stay, Morgan became very sick, and the only available doctor was a medic with the French Foreign Legion. Under the doctor's care, Morgan slowly got better, and we returned to France a few days later. This brush with fate did nothing to calm the growing apprehension that I felt about my newborn son. Soon after, we flew to Chapel Hill, NC, to introduce Morgan to my mom and dad, who was a professor at the University of North Carolina in the School of Public Health. They were thrilled to spend time with our beautiful blue-eyed boy. Morgan was destined to become a world traveler. Within the first month of his life, he had visited three continents: Europe, Africa, and North America.

All four of our children were born in Montpellier, including our baby Chelsea, who survived for only two days. I had been in the hospital on an IV for two months with placenta previa before Chelsea's birth, during which time Morgan stayed with my mother-in-law. I could not take care of him, and it was challenging to leave him. I spent my days in the hospital bed sick with worry, imagining that Morgan thought that I had suddenly abandoned him. He was my best buddy.

Despite the care that I was receiving at the hospital, I could not hold onto Chelsea any longer. She came into the world by C-section on January 21st, 1991. My water had broken several days earlier, and her lungs were crushed before she was finally delivered. I knew that she was in distress because I felt her kick less and less as her birth approached. I tried desperately but unsuccessfully to get the nurses to do something to help her. Chelsea survived on a respirator for only two days. Because of my Caesarian, I could not cry or mourn her passing; the slightest contraction of my stomach was agonizing. I was released from the hospital a few days after her birth.

It was a huge relief to finally get home to my sweet Morgan. He was the reason I was able to heal. However, with the passing of Chelsea, I began to feel that I had one foot here on earth and one foot on the other side with my tiny angel. Later, after Chelsea transitioned, we were fortunate to add two beautiful daughters to our family: Alix in 1992, and Christine in 1995.

When Morgan was seven, we moved with him and our daughters to the United States. During Morgan's childhood, he was in a hurry to do everything. He learned to walk at 7 months and seemed to only have one speed when he was a toddler: a fast-paced run. I was even compelled to have him wear a harness with a leash for a year to keep from losing him, much to the dismay of my French friends and family. Morgan hurried to grow taller and bigger than all the other kids in his classes. My big boy seemed to burst at the seams with energy and enthusiasm. He also raced to join and excel at many sports. He studied Judo at age four and earned his black belt in Taekwondo at age eleven. In high school, Morgan was a defensive lineman on his high school football team, and at 6'7" and 280 pounds, he was essential to the coach and the team. His athleticism and leadership skills in both football and track earned him a Marine Corps Distinguished Scholar-Athlete Award. These activities calmed him down and reined in some of his extra energy.

When Morgan graduated from high school and left for the University of Arizona, my world abruptly tilted. Suddenly, his enormous presence no longer filled our home. We all loved watching as Morgan burst through the kitchen door to grab us for a bear hug, sometimes forcing me to walk backward as he held onto me. Or when he would sprint down the hallway, jumping to hit each archway on the way back to his room. And we would laugh hysterically as he performed silly handshakes with his sisters. At the University of Arizona, because of his gregarious personality and massive height, it was natural that the cheer squad recruited Morgan. The team aptly nicknamed Morgan 'Big Bear' for the enormous bear hugs he gave.

Morgan already spoke two languages, English and French. After spending his sophomore year in Nanjing, China, majoring in East Asian Studies/Chinese, he was determined to learn Chinese and become trilingual. While there, Morgan participated in pre-Olympic games through Nanjing Normal University. As he was almost twice the size of his competition, it was no surprise when he placed first in shotput out of students from thirty participating universities.

The summer before Morgan passed, he spent six weeks studying and traveling in France. His fluency in French and his caring nature led him to become the pseudo-protector of the other kids in the program. As such, Morgan regularly accompanied the girls who lived in unsafe neighborhoods back to their apartments.

We met up with Morgan at the end of his stay in Paris and flew to Montpellier to spend time with our family. It would be the last time he would see his French relatives. Memories from that lazy summer are enduring and beautiful for the rest of us. One evening, Morgan lingered by the pool at a friend's home as the sun was setting. He recorded his own version of 'I Believe I Can Fly' on his Blackberry phone on that beautiful twilit evening. He was a huge fan of Michael Jordan and had watched the movie that made the song famous,

'Space Jam,' at least sixty times. We found the recording on his phone after he passed. Hearing it play from time to time on the radio became a way to validate that Morgan was near.

After a long, peaceful summer, Morgan returned to study in Nanjing, China, on August 30th, 2009. While packing for his second trip to Nanjing, we attempted to stuff five months' worth of clothing and supplies into one enormous suitcase. Morgan turned to me and said: "Mom, I don't think that I will be coming home from China this time." Even though I had suffered from premonitions about Morgan all his life, this was a shock. After composing myself, I responded that he had no real reason to leave; he could stay and return to Tucson instead. But Morgan was ready to go. He calmly put his hand on my shoulder and said: "Mom, I'll be fine." Two months later, Morgan passed of severe altitude sickness at the Base Camp of Mount Everest. He didn't lie. I now know that he truly is 'fine.'

October 20th, 2009, started like any other fall day in Cave Creek, AZ. Two days prior, Morgan had left to spend fall break in Tibet with thirteen other students from his study abroad program. I had just arrived from a Tuesday afternoon yoga class and received a call from Morgan's program director. He told me that Morgan was in distress and that the students were descending the mountain to get him to safety.

I quickly called Colin, Morgan's roommate, and best friend in China. As soon as Colin answered, he told me that the situation didn't look good. Morgan had stopped breathing, and they were attempting CPR. Colin was not sure that Morgan would make it. I was terrified but knew that Morgan needed to hear my voice. I wanted to pour all the love and gratitude I felt for my beautiful son through the receiver as he lay on the cold Tibetan ground. I asked Colin to put the phone up to his ear. I told Morgan that we loved him, that we were proud of him, and not to be afraid. At that very instant, I felt Morgan hug me from the inside. To this day, I still cannot correctly explain this sensation. It was incredible; I felt a warm, calming feeling wash through me. That moment was utterly life changing. I later found out that this event was called a Shared Death Experience. Through it, Morgan comforted me and reassured me that he would always be with me. In an instant, I knew that love never dies.

Through the years, I've been told by several mediums that Chelsea was the first person to meet Morgan during his transition. This explanation made sense to me. As she knew the ropes, Chelsea was able to grab Morgan's hand and lead him to me. Morgan and Chelsea have stayed with me throughout my healing journey. And whenever I feel sad, I can always count on Morgan to hug me from the inside. Moreover, Morgan has since let us know that if he hadn't transitioned at the Base Camp of Mount Everest, it would have happened on the I-10 coming home from the U of A to Cave Creek. There was nothing that we could have done to stop his transition.

Although Morgan's passing forever changed the lives of everyone in my family, knowing where he was and that he was safe and happy reassured me. It helped me become an anchor for my husband and daughters. We learned to navigate our new lives without Morgan's vast, loving presence in our family. A family friend gifted me with Dr. Raymond Moody's book, Life After Life, and I gratefully read it in the days immediately following Morgan's transition. I realized that there was scientific evidence to support the connection I felt with Morgan. Signs and validations have reassured us many times since his passing that he is with us. I have chosen a few moments that resonate deeply.

After Morgan's passing, I desperately wanted to communicate with him. I had never been to a psychic medium, and I didn't see how it could be possible to reach my son this way until something extraordinary happened one week after his passing. I had been practicing yoga at a studio for many years, and Morgan had sometimes attended with me. Earlier that day, Angie Bayliss, the studio owner, had interviewed a psychic medium, Susanne Wilson, who was looking for rental space. During her conversation with Angie, Susanne not only connected with Morgan, but she also communicated his personality and mannerisms. Through Susanne, Morgan gave Angie numerous validations. She said she was being shown a big teddy bear and a bottle of Captain Morgan. She saw a young man shouting through a megaphone that he was 'fine'. Morgan had used a cheerleading megaphone that sat on display at his memorial service and is still in a place of honor in his room. Susanne also saw him on a mountain, lying on his back. She saw a black box next to his ear and understood that he had listened intently but had been unable to speak. He told Susanne to say, "Mom, I heard everything you said, and I love you back." It was a tremendous validation to know Morgan had heard me as Colin held the phone up to his ear. His response through Susanne was typical of what Morgan always answered, day after day, for years before he passed.

Susanne also told Angie that Morgan and his two roommates in China were like a 'band of brothers.' Morgan was close to all the students on the student exchange, but his two roommates were especially significant. Colin and Matt accompanied Morgan's body to Lhasa. They waited with him until my husband could receive a visa to enter Tibet six days later. Perhaps the most important message communicated by Susanne was that we would receive a unique rock from the place that Morgan transitioned. Susanne sketched it for us, showing that the stone was split in two. A month later, Morgan's roommate Colin arrived at our home, carrying a bouquet of my favorite flowers. With it, he brought the two halves of Morgan's rock from the desolate tract of Tibetan countryside where he passed. It looked just like the picture that Susanne drew.

My husband Cyril returned to work in China soon after Morgan's passing. After waiting for three excruciating days in Chengdu for a Tibetan visa, he had traveled to Tibet to retrieve Morgan's body. It was nearly impossible to bring Morgan home because of legislative roadblocks. Still, he was finally able to do so thanks to his dedication and meaningful friendships in China.

Cyril had visited Morgan in Nanjing several times while he was studying there, so being back in China after Morgan transitioned was especially hard for him. On one particular morning, he was on his way to the airport to fly from Hong Kong to Beijing. It was very early, perhaps 5:00 am, and most of the city was still sleeping. Cyril sat in a taxi, thinking of Morgan, and missing him more than ever. Cantonese music played softly on the radio. Suddenly, Cyril recognized a familiar tune: "I used to think that I could not go on, and life was nothing but an awful song. But now I know the meaning of true love, I'm leaning on the everlasting arms." It was the song that Morgan had recorded while in France, 'I Believe I Can Fly.' Here it was, playing on his taxi's radio on the outskirts of Hong Kong, on a lonely road leading to the airport. This decisive sign lifted Cyril's spirits and gave him strength for the remainder of his trip. He was confident that Morgan was with him.

Morgan and Chelsea send signs every day to let me know that they are still right here. One of the best signs we have received was on Morgan's 30th birthday when we hiked to the bench dedicated to him and Chelsea in the Spur Cross Recreation Area. As we walked towards the bench, I told Morgan that it would be wonderful to get a big sign from him. Very soon after, we spotted a bobcat up ahead in the middle of the path as we made our way through the beautiful desert. Seeing the bobcat was significant because the University of Arizona mascot is a Wildcat. The bobcat seemed to want to stay with us and approached us to within three feet. We took multiple pictures of the beautiful cat as it wound its way through the desert flowers, seemingly purring at us. My husband and I had no doubt that this majestic feline was a gift from our son.

My two daughters both feel Morgan's presence in their lives. They realize that knowing our children in spirit are happy, healthy, and whole helps us move forward and heal. Therefore, they have spent the past 11 years supporting my work at Helping Parents Heal, welcoming parents to monthly meetings with hugs, smiles, and genuine love. I know that the kindness and compassion that they have provided have helped the two of them on their own healing journeys.

Christine often has lifelike dreams of Morgan and knows that he is with her. Alix connects with Morgan through meditation and even believes that Morgan saved her life. In 2012, while she was studying at Sciences Po in Paris, she attended a party with her cousin, Anne-Sophie, in a neighborhood far from her home in St. Germain. She had taken migraine medicine before leaving, and after a few glasses of champagne, she started to feel dizzy. She threw up in the bathroom of the bar and told Anne-Sophie that she was going home. In her confusion, she forgot to grab her coat on the way out.

Wearing only a sleeveless cocktail dress, she embarked on her journey home under gently falling snow. Arriving at the curb, she jumped into the first available taxi. After a few stoplights, she looked to her left and did not recognize the person sitting next to her. She opened the taxi door and vomited again, then crawled out and stood freezing on the street corner. Staring at the street names painted on the building walls, she realized that she was lost. She attempted to call friends with her cellphone as the street names began to blur together. She was unable to reach anyone, and no one knew where she was.

Alix's next recollection was of being shaken awake by her two roommates. It was morning, and she was back in her bed, safe and sound. The girls had a flight to Portugal leaving at 7 am and needed to hurry to the airport. Alix sorted through her memories, trying to piece together how she had made it home. One of her roommates, who had stayed home the night before, remembered hearing the front door burst open at 3 am. Later, when her second roommate arrived, the door was still ajar. The girls lived in a 9th-floor penthouse apartment that was only accessible by a winding staircase. After exiting a taxi headed in the wrong direction, Alix last remembered sitting down in the snow, kilometers from home. She is confident that Morgan carried her safely home.

Many of the validations that we receive come from Morgan's friends. While on the cheerleading team at U of A, Morgan befriended Dan, aka the school mascot Wilbur the Wildcat. Dan later became a firefighter. Once, when a fire was raging above him in a home, Dan helped a fellow firefighter remove a car from the garage below. His friend put the car into neutral, and Dan was to push it out of the garage. Suddenly, Dan felt someone hugging him tightly around his chest and pulling him forcibly backward. He said that it felt as though Morgan was giving him an enormous bear hug from behind. As Dan was yanked back, a huge air conditioning unit fell through from the floor above. The firefighter who was sitting in the car saw the whole thing and exclaimed, "Dude-what just happened?" Without a doubt, Dan knew that Morgan had saved his life.

After Chelsea passed, I realized that there is more to our existence than this one physical lifetime. I knew she was not gone, and I was ultimately able to survive her passing with the help of my son Morgan. When Morgan passed in 2009 and gave me that tremendous hug, I was determined to learn all I could about the Afterlife. I needed to understand where Morgan was, who he was with, and what he did all day.

Helping Parents Heal grew out of a Facebook group I started in October 2009, one week after my son Morgan transitioned. I knew that I was not the only parent experiencing these signs from our children, and I wanted to share with people who understood. After joining forces with Mark Ireland and with the help of Doryce Norwood, our pro bono attorney, Helping Parents Heal became a nonprofit in 2012. It has far exceeded its humble beginnings. We now offer support and healing to Shining Light Parents on a worldwide basis. The goal of the support meetings conducted by affiliate groups is to let parents know that their kids are not gone. They are still right here.

Helping Parents Heal now has over 130 affiliate groups in the US, Canada, the United Kingdom, South Africa, India, Australia, and New Zealand. We also have Caring Listeners, parents who volunteer to lend a healing ear to newer members. Dr. Mark Pitstick and Lynn Hollahan (Devon's Shining Light Mom) lead this inspiring group of parents. Carol Allen, Tyler's Shining Light mom, is one of our Caring Listeners and leads several affiliate groups. Irene Vouvalides, Carly's Shining Light Mom, joined our group and immediately volunteered as an affiliate leader.

Then soon after Irene joined, she suggested that Helping Parents Heal host a conference. Planning an event this size is no small task, but Irene was persistent. Following more than a year of hard work and transcontinental phone calls to coordinate the event, we proudly held our First Helping Parents Heal Conference in Scottsdale, Arizona, in 2018. The sold-out event hosted 500 parents and 30 presenters. A dozen Shining Light Parents volunteered to help the incredible conference run without a hitch. Ironically, and unsurprisingly, the staff at the hotel reported that our guests appeared to be the happiest that they had ever hosted. We will be holding our Second HPH Conference in Phoenix in August 2022, and we plan to welcome 1000 parents. All of the proceeds from the sale of this book will go towards the conference.

Please know that you are not alone. We share this journey, and we understand. We are all in this together, and together, we will help each other heal.

-Written by Morgan's Shining Light Mom, President and Co-Founder of Helping Parents Heal, Affiliate Leader of HPH Phoenix/Scottsdale, HPH Caring Listener and Newsletter Editor, Elizabeth Boisson

Susan Marie Giesemann-Babich

My husband, Ty, hiked in a melancholy mood on the wooded trail in Virginia. He and his daughter, Susan, had shared this experience many times, but they never would again. Her death at age 27 had cut short their dream of hiking the Appalachian Trail together. Suddenly, two fingers pressed firmly against his arm, causing him to turn around. He looked to see who was trying to get his attention, but there was no one in sight. The former Navy destroyer captain lowered himself onto a nearby log as the tears flowed. He could not deny Susan's presence.

This was Ty's first physical experience of Susan's presence since she and his unborn grandson, Liam Tyler, were killed by a lightning strike. It was far from the first sign that Susan had sent to let us know that she and all those who pass are *still right here*.

Ty and I were together the week after Susan's funeral when the television went on in our hotel room while we sat twenty feet away on the balcony. The timing of this inexplicable event was uncanny. At that very moment I was reading an explanation by a medium that those in spirit often make their presence known by turning electronics on and off.

Ty and I both witnessed the butterfly that followed our boat at sea later that same week.

Butterflies on the ocean are rare, and this one fluttered past us just as I was reading how butterflies are used in unusual ways by those in spirit to signal that they are around.

I was the only one present when Susan dropped into my morning meditation for an unforgettable Father's Day gift. Sitting in the silence was a daily practice I initiated after Susan's transition in hopes of connecting directly with her. My efforts paid off that Sunday morning when she spoke to me in full sentences in her own voice.

I asked her to share with me things going on in her biological mother's life that I didn't know about. This way, when I told others about this oh-so-special visit, the evidence would validate her presence. "Her cat is sick, she has Christmas lights up inside the house year-round, and she has a funny story about a ladder," Susan told me.

When her mother confirmed all three of these items, we celebrated. The evidence backed up Susan's loving messages for all of us and her assurance that she and Liam were happy.

It's no surprise that Susan communicated so clearly once I learned to attune to the spirit world. She used to love talking to people of all ages, and she left everyone with a smile. Her spunky "I can do anything" attitude led her to excel in the U.S. Marine Corps, graduating third in the challenging Sergeant's Course and earning her flight crew wings.

She loved her husband, and they were thriving in their first home. Were it not for the bolt of lightning that struck her as she was crossing the flight line at her duty station at Marine Corps Air Station Cherry Point, North Carolina, we have no doubt she would have been a fantastic mother. She had already proved her maternal abilities as mom to three dogs and a cat.

Did Susan know at a soul level about her impending transition? Yes, of course. The soul knows many things that don't filter down into our human awareness. Susan came to me quite clearly in a vivid dream two days before she passed and told me that she and the baby were fine. One might brush off such a timely message as mere coincidence. There is no other explanation, however, than "the soul knows," for the fact that three months before she passed, Susan named her new puppy Thor, after the Norse god of thunder and lightning. And her other dog at the time? Athena, the Greek goddess of lightning.

Such "No Other Explanation" stories are the norm in our lives now. Susan's passing was the catalyst for a spiritual journey I never saw coming. Today I know that those who pass are still part of our lives. They exist in a non-physical form that is creative, intelligent, and very much aware of family and friends still in physical form.

When Susan passed, I had no idea that we are both human and souls arising from the one Unified Field of Consciousness. Her father and I served full careers as U.S. Navy officers. I was quite left-brained—a necessary quality in my job as aide to the head of the U.S. military, the Chairman of the Joint Chiefs of Staff. Discussions about spirits and our eternal nature were not part of my life at that time.

Seeing Susan's body at her funeral changed all that. Suddenly, I knew beyond any doubt that there is something very much alive within each of us which departs its temporary vessel at the time of death. Standing beside her casket, looking down at something so detached from my vibrant stepdaughter, I made it my new mission to connect with the part of Susan that could not die.

Reading books on the Afterlife is immensely helpful to shift one's belief system and open one's awareness to a greater reality. Nothing can compare, however, with the personal experience of lifting the veil that separates these apparently separate worlds. Through a daily practice of sitting in the silence with the intention of accessing Susan and higher levels of consciousness, I ultimately succeeded in my goal. It did not happen overnight. It took dedication and commitment, and a refusal to give up.

As a result of these efforts, along the way I enjoyed adventures in consciousness beyond my expectations. Most gratifying of all, not only was I able to connect quite clearly with Susan, but with others' loved ones as well. My experiences showed that one does not have to be aware of this innate ability from birth to awaken it.

Today, I dedicate my work to Susan. My journey from military officer to medium is detailed in my memoir, *Messages of Hope,* as well as in a documentary on YouTube and Amazon Prime by the same name. To now be able to provide hope and healing to those in their darkest hour and show them a path to spiritual awakening is one of the unexpected silver linings of Susan's transition.

Another unanticipated blessing is the deep friendships Ty and I have forged with other Shining Light Parents. Through our shared sorrow, we now enjoy a depth of connection that goes far beyond normal friendly acquaintances. Through the Helping Parents Heal organization, we have bonded with other couples in a way that few humans experience.

My book, *Still Right Here*, details a miraculous week spent in close quarters aboard a boat with four such couples that was unmarred by the slightest ripple of discontent or petty quibbling. The palpable love we experienced reflected our awareness that the eight of us were accompanied at every moment of that special vacation by our children across the veil.

Such claims might sound strange to those who are new to this journey. The ongoing magical validations that our children give us to show us they are still part of our lives gives us the confidence to speak openly of their presence.

When I first became aware of the spirit world and the ability to connect with those who have passed, I wanted to shout it from the rooftops.

"Don't ever say you have proof of the Afterlife," someone once warned me. This well-meaning friend was trying to protect me from skeptics, who can be quite harsh in their criticism.

I understand skepticism. In the absence of evidence, the existence of a non-physical world that is as solid to its inhabitants as ours appears to us seems far-fetched and even fanciful.

But more than a decade of receiving jaw-dropping validations from two-way conversations with clever, creative, humorous, sentient souls has left me with no doubt whatsoever that death is not the end of life.

Today, thanks to Susan, to those many souls who have trusted me with their messages, and most especially, to a young man named Wolf[1], I have gone from skepticism to *knowing* that we don't "lose" our loved ones. I *guarantee* you that consciousness is not dependent upon the brain and that your loved ones who have passed are still part of your life.

Susan had a large tattoo on her hip. It depicted a colorful phoenix with majestic wings. The tattoo is yet another portent of a life that burned brightly and was snuffed out in a powerful burst of light. But the phoenix represents far more than death. It stands as a symbol of life and rebirth ... of rising from the ashes and moving forward as the eternal souls we all are.

I know that Susan joins me in assuring you that your efforts to connect with your beloved friends and family members across the veil are not in vain. Your prayers, your heartfelt conversations uttered silently or aloud, are not holding them back but are heard and so very much appreciated.

-Written by Susan's Shining Light Stepmom, Suzanne Giesemann, Messenger of Hop

---

[1] See my book, *Wolf's Message* for undeniable proof that the soul is aware and connected to the greater reality.

Tyler John Allen

On July 8, 1995, my beautiful baby boy Tyler Allen entered our world. He gave us quite the scare when he inhaled meconium into his lungs during birth. Unfortunately, he had to stay in intensive care for fourteen days. Once he was ready to leave the hospital, he was a perfectly healthy and happy baby and incredibly easy to raise.

Tyler was mature and highly empathic from a very young age; unfortunately, this often-created heartache for him. His feelings would quickly get hurt when he saw someone mistreated; Tyler wouldn't hesitate to stand up to a bully. He always had numerous friends, giving of himself, loving, and putting others first. One of his teachers called me one day, praising Tyler for precisely that.

Baseball and soccer were his passion in elementary school; his interests changed once he entered high school. He loved BMX bikes, mountain bikes, and dirt bikes. An outdoor enthusiast, he also enjoyed snowboarding, boating, fishing, and camping.

Tyler loved the girls and always had a girlfriend. Most of his relationships lasted quite a while; his longest relationship continued for two years.

Adventure called to him constantly. He was always in a hurry. Whenever there was somewhere to go or something to do, he was the first one up. "Let's go, let's go, he would say." He wanted to experience everything life had to offer.

He was so grateful and always expressed his gratitude for the people in his life. He once posted a picture on Facebook of his family, including aunts, uncles, and cousins, to say, "I couldn't ask for a better family." He later tagged me in another pic with his dad to express how lucky he was and that his parents were his best friends.

Nature was his sanctuary. He would hike a mountain and sit there to watch the sunset. He appreciated the mountains, the desert, the forest, and the beach.

Once high school ended, Tyler moved to Flagstaff and attended NAU for a semester; he was excited to live in the snow and have the ability to snowboard often. His stay there was short-lived; he missed his family and group of friends. Tyler also told me within weeks of starting NAU that he wasn't a college boy and wanted to attend MMI (Motorcycle Mechanics Institute). He eventually wanted to open a custom motorcycle shop. I was not happy about this. I didn't want my nineteen-year-old on a motorcycle; however, my husband reminded me that he was a grown man, and I needed to allow him to pursue his dreams.

I worried about Tyler constantly. Not only because he rode a motorcycle, but there had always been something, deep inside of me, that knew his life would be cut short. I would push the thoughts away; however, they were there. I would think, "No, something like that couldn't happen to me; I would never survive." Tyler also made a strange comment one day regarding a girl he was dating; he said, "I'm not sure this should be my last girlfriend." Of course, my initial thought was, "You don't have to marry her; you are only nineteen." After he made the statement, I noticed a puzzled look in his eyes just as the words left his mouth, "That was a weird thing to say, huh, mom?" I know now that both of our souls knew. As humans, we cannot possibly comprehend something so devastating. When I think back to my early twenties, I can also clearly recall saying to a boyfriend that I couldn't imagine losing a child. I wasn't married then; I didn't have children at the time, but yet, this thought occurred to me. Why? Because my soul already knew.

Although I grew up Catholic, attending catholic schools for many years, I wasn't sure that I believed in God or an Afterlife before

Tyler's passing. The longer I lived, the less I believed, contributing to my fear of death. I had so many life questions.

On May 13, 2015, tragedy struck, and my life forever changed when a woman's careless driving caused her to cut in front of Tyler while he was riding his motorcycle. He was rushed to the hospital by ambulance; he passed away on May 14, 2015.

Shortly after that, I met Elizabeth Boisson, the President and Co-Founder of Helping Parents Heal. Elizabeth came to Tyler's service because her daughter Christine knew Tyler. She introduced herself to me. Elizabeth became my earth angel. She opened me up to a world I didn't know existed. She gave me the support, tools, and resources to help me move forward when I didn't think I could survive or ever experience joy again. I read every book that Elizabeth recommended that I could get my hands on regarding the Afterlife. I would search the internet, looking for something, anything to comfort me. I came across videos from people who had had a near-death experience. I found Jefferey Olsen and Dr. Mary Neal. Their stories are remarkable. Recognizing the signs from our loved ones, afterlife communication, soul plans, and reincarnation were some of the many things I discovered. My research took a lot of work and much time; however, it was well worth it.

I had proof that there was no denying this new reality when I saw Tyler's reflection in a picture of my husband's motorcycle helmet. The photo was taken during Tyler's celebration of life. I knew then that Tyler was there all along, and he saw all the love surrounding him. The photo began to get passed around to everyone. Even recently, I have received texts asking me if I could resend the picture of Tyler's face.

Grocery shopping was always a painful reminder that I didn't need to shop for Tyler's favorite items. I decided to go to Safeway instead of Fry's, hoping it would help to change my surroundings. As I walked down the chip aisle, I glanced at one of Tyler's favorite snacks, Nacho Cheese Doritos. I felt the tears coming, and the bag instantly fell to my feet. I was the only one in the aisle! Tyler knocked it down to say hi.

Shortly after Tyler passed away, there was another instance when my husband Tony was putting gas into his truck. His diesel truck typically takes at least $60.00 to fill. The dollar amount stopped calculating at $20.03; however, the gas nozzle continued to pour into his vehicle for another few minutes. Once it stopped, Tony walked into the gas station to notify the attendant that there must be something wrong. He explained that it only charged him $20.03, but he felt that it had to be closer to $60.00. The attendant shrugged his shoulders and said, "Well, you only owe $20.03."

Once Tony got into his truck, he called to tell me what had just happened. We both laughed, and I said, "Tyler must want to save us money." I later sent Elizabeth a text to tell her about it, and she immediately looked up the meaning of angel number 2003. "Angel Number 2003 tells us that learning our life lessons can be joyful when we focus upon all that we gain as a consequence of our increased understanding, knowledge, and wisdom. Your current experiences are presenting you with wonderful opportunities for spiritual awareness and growth and bringing you important life lessons. Once you accept and understand these lessons, outdated patterns will leave your life to be replaced with wonderful new opportunities and experiences." This message came at the perfect time. I had very recently started to learn about soul plans and life lessons. The statement also let me know that I need to use my talents to uplift, enlighten and benefit myself and the world around me. I need to strive to help others. How appropriate! I genuinely believe that helping others is my life's journey. I find so much joy as a Cave Creek Affiliate Leader and Caring Listener for Helping Parents Heal.

I highly recommend a suitable medium. Our first reading following Tyler's passing was with Susanne Wilson. It was phenomenal, to say the least. She knew things that no one could have known. Once she finished her opening prayer, she immediately said, "Does May 14 mean something to you?" "Yes." Susanne continued, "There is a young male here, he is on a tricked-out motorcycle, and he is asking, mom, remember when?" She suddenly stopped and said, "Oh my God, you lost a son?" Of course, my tears started to flow. I couldn't speak, but my husband answered, "Yes." Susanne then said, "Well, I don't know anything about you other than your first name, but he knows everything." Well, he sure did because, for the next hour, the validations kept coming. It was incredible! I couldn't believe my ears. Even if Susanne had known my entire story, which she did not--my sister intentionally paid her in cash--no one could have known some of the validations she gave us. Tyer said over and over, "I am not gone; I am not gone."

Susanne said, "You found a shiny rock on your couch." I wasn't aware of any rock; however, my husband immediately responded, "Yes, I did; it was in the pillows." Susanne responded, "That was a rock he found in Sedona; he was leaning back on the couch with his feet on the coffee table when it fell out." She said, "Now he is messing with you mom, he says, get your feet off the coffee table." Then she said, "He is laughing." "I'm kidding, mom; you were not like that; you just wanted me around." Yes! That's precisely what I would tell my friends when they would complain about how messy their kids were or how they wouldn't clean up after themselves. I would say, "I don't worry about those things; I want my kids around. They will be out on their own someday, and then I will miss these days."

Susanne asked, "Who is Jack?" "Jack is my young nephew.", I responded. "Does Jack have a heart issue?" She asked. I answered, "Yes, he had open-heart surgery last year when he was four."

Suzanne then said, "Well, Tyler is watching over him. He doesn't want you or his parents to worry."

We had an hour-long conversation with our son. Following my reading, I went home and took out all of Tyler's photos that I had put away following his passing. I had found them too painful to look at, but now they are all over my home again.

Since my reading with Susanne, I have had many others, all wonderful! I cannot express enough the healing that occurs.
I do not doubt that Tyler sent Elizabeth my way. He knew his mom needed help! I am forever grateful to her and Helping Parents Heal.

There have been so many amazing, and to some, who do not understand, unbelievable signs. My sisters, parents, cousins, and friends have received beautiful signs and messages to prove Tyler is here. The relief and happiness that take over are inexplicable. Please don't misunderstand, I will always miss his physical presence, but the fact remains that he is not gone, and he is happy. Isn't this what we want for our children--to know that they are ok and happy?
I found a journal while cleaning Tyler's room months after he gained his angel wings. The only statement written in the entire diary was, "I know two things, I exist, and God exists." In my opinion more proof that our soul is aware.

As time continued, I discovered a love for yoga and meditation. These practices helped me to raise my vibration, so connecting became easier. I learned about Reiki, automatic writing, and communicating with a pendulum. I found peace; I found happiness. My son has not left; I know without a doubt that he has simply stepped into another room. My relationship with him continues, and it is as strong as ever. I now connect with my son from the other side every day. I hear him constantly as he guides and helps me. Music is a wonderful way to communicate. Listen to the words; if it appears as though your loved one is speaking to you, trust that they are. I have one foot here and one foot there. My family will always leave an empty chair for holidays and major events. We also continue to celebrate Tyler on his angel date and birthday by releasing butterflies on his angelversary and baking a beautiful cake for him on his heavenly birthday. Tyler was and still is a beautiful old soul.

As my dear friend Elizabeth says, "Look for the collateral beauty in your story." I recognize the silver lining here. I no longer fear death; in fact, I look forward to it when my time comes. I have learned everything I can about the Afterlife and the fantastic world that we call heaven. I have surrendered to my journey with no expectations and found pleasure in the simplest things; the smell of my coffee in the morning and sitting in nature while the birds chirp.

I live in the present with Tyler and work very hard not to dwell on the past or worry about the future. I am incredibly grateful. I am blessed and have a lot to be thankful for. I have met some of the most loving people on this journey. I have always loved, but I have learned to love more. I have always had compassion; however, I have found more compassion towards others. I have forgiven the woman who caused Tyler's accident. She has her own journey. Holding on to the anger serves no purpose and only hurts me. We all have our stories. We all have our challenges; we are here to learn; we are here to grow. I choose love. I choose happiness. I know Tyler wants me to be happy.

If you are interested in hearing more about my healing journey and all of the excellent signs I have received, you will find it all in my book, *Tyler Lives, Mom, I'm Not Gone*.

-Written by Tyler's Shining Light Mom and Helping Parents Heal Board Member, HPH Cave Creek Affiliate Leader, HPH Book Club Affiliate Leader, Presenter and HPH Caring Listener, Carol Allen

Carly Elizabeth Hughes

Carly Elizabeth Hughes was born on her due date, October 10, 1988. She always lived her life to the fullest, at full speed, exhausting anyone who chose to "have an adventure" with her, as she loved to say. Her college friends shared stories at her memorial service about how Carly was always in charge. At a college party, she decided everyone had to address each other by their middle name only; of course, they listened, because Carly said so! She would wake her roommates on weekends early in the morning to travel to the beaches in Massachusetts instead of sleeping in after a party. When she was in high school, I would often wake to find that she had been up all night at her sewing machine, making a dress or a slipcover for the loveseat in her room.

Now that I look back, I often wonder if she subconsciously knew her time on earth would be brief, and she needed to experience life as fully as possible.

We had the best time during her visits to potential colleges. While visiting the University of Richmond, where she was offered a partial scholarship, Carly let the admissions director know after our tour that she couldn't possibly attend a school whose mascot was a spider; she was petrified of them. She fell in love with Boston College the minute she set foot on campus, and she loved to tell people she decided on BC because it was only an eight-minute cab ride to her favorite store--Bloomingdale's.

While at Boston College, Carly participated in and then led a service trip to the oldest African American elementary school in the Mississippi Valley, Holy Family Early Learning Academy. She came back from those service trips determined that one day she would teach there. While she did not get that chance, we have supported the school through the foundation I have created in her honor and memory: Carly's Kids--A Foundation for Education.

She loved Boston, and after graduating from Boston College with a degree in education and a secondary degree in math, she decided to make Boston her home. She navigated the T in Boston as if she had been riding it her entire life and loved living in the North End with the fabulous Italian restaurants and pastry shops.

After her college graduation, Carly and I flew into Barcelona and traveled to Venice, Rome, Florence, Tuscany, and Dubrovnik, Croatia. She had fallen in love with Venice after spending a month abroad there during her junior year fulfilling her Fine Arts requirements. Carly was fluent in Spanish and understood Italian. Her knowledge of the Vaporetto water taxi system was amazing, and she took me to all of her favorite places in Venice.

While we were dining one evening together at an outdoor café, two waiters were flirting with her and speaking Italian to each other. Little did they know Carly understood them. She then informed them she would not marry either one of them just so they could come to the United States. (They both turned bright red after that!)

She was a loyal friend, a loving and kind soul who loved children and animals. She would send me pictures of herself with animals in shelters begging me to adopt a dog or a cat since she had a strict no-pet policy in her apartment in Boston.

After Carly's Celebration of Life, a friend reminded me of a question I had asked her when Carly was four years old: would I still be a mother if something happened to Carly? That nagging fear was always with me, and at Carly's college graduation, I remarked to my husband that I had worried all those years, and here she was graduating from college, ready to begin a new chapter of her life. How foolish I had been to worry for all of these years, I silently thought to myself.

A little more than a year later, Carly was diagnosed with esophageal-gastric cancer. She left this Earth on February 17, 2013, after a brief and horrific battle with this cancer, unheard of in someone only 24 years old. Carly was the youngest person ever diagnosed at NY Columbia Presbyterian Hospital with esophageal-gastric cancer. During the four months of radiation, chemotherapy, multiple surgeries, and blood transfusions, Carly never once complained. She took control as best she could by memorizing her vitals, times for her blood draws, tests, and meds. She befriended every person she met at NY Columbia Presbyterian Hospital, where she was treated. She always had a smile on her face, thanking each member of her extended medical team. I never once let the thought cross my mind that she would not survive this, believing in the power of prayer and positive thinking. God would never "take" my only child from me was a frequent and repetitive thought. I know now that destiny determines our fate regardless of the best possible treatment and care given by renowned physicians. I do believe now that your arrival and exit dates are predetermined.

I did not think I could survive her passing, nor did I want to. I was newly married, and my husband's first wife had passed from pancreatic cancer years earlier. My mantra became "Tony cannot be twice-widowed," and those words kept me from joining Carly. I was lost for months in the deep dark hole of grief, spending my days sobbing, curled on our couch. I truly wanted to die. The days seemed endless, followed by sleepless nights; I felt utterly lost and helpless.

My sister felt Carly's presence almost immediately and received some amazing signs very soon after Carly's passing. One evening Judi asked Carly to please help her and send a sign so she could share it with me. In the browser's search engine on my sister's phone, the words appeared "Heaven looks a lot like a mall." Anyone who knows Carly knew that shopping and spending time at a mall were one of her favorite pastimes. But at that point in my grief, I would not have been able to recognize a sign if it hit me over my head. I wasn't sure what to make of my sister's message, even though I know it was miraculous when I look back now.

I had slowly started crawling out of my rabbit hole of grief when I met my now-dear friend Beth whose son Sean had passed in a car accident in 2004. Beth lived in Hawaii, and one of my girlfriends was in Beth's spin class at The Four Seasons Resort on the Big Island of Hawaii, where they were vacationing. She told Beth about Carly and me after Beth shared her story during that class of Sean's passing in a car accident. My friend Sally returned home from Hawaii with a letter from Beth and a beautiful bracelet made of crystals in angel shapes. I called Beth, and we began a daily ritual of phone calls that offered me friendship and hope. A six-hour time difference separated us, and I cherished Beth's calls on her before-dawn drive to work in Hawaii, where it was late morning on the east coast where I lived. I had found someone who had experienced what I was living with; I could see she was functioning, living her life joyfully, always keeping her son close to her heart. Beth helped me find the strength to carry on. I devoured books about The Afterlife, spirituality, and works written by mediums. I set my sights on connecting with Carly.

After months of research and watching an HBO documentary titled The Afterlife Experiments, I learned about George Anderson. Dr. Gary Schwartz tested mediums George Anderson, John Edwards, Suzanne Northrop, Laurie Campbell, and Anne Gehman in this documentary. Seven months after Carly's passing I scheduled a reading with George for my sister Judi and me, and we made the journey to a conference room in a hotel in Long Island, NY. Before that reading, I had set an intention to hopefully learn that Carly had not been frightened or alone when she passed. These worries had consumed me when I thought of her passing, and I had been sick over the possibilities.

Judi and I sat across from George, who immediately sensed the presence of a young female who had passed. He looked at me and said, "You have a daughter who has passed, and she wants you to stop obsessing about her passing; it was as easy as walking through a doorway.... your mother was there to greet her". So many validations came through during that session from Carly and our beloved mother, who passed four years before Carly.

This reading showed me that our loved ones who have passed are always with us and very much alive in the hereafter. Messages came through that could not be found in any search done about my sister or me. Our loved ones in spirit still exist. I felt a lightness that I had not experienced since that Sunday morning in February when Carly passed.

After reading Dr. Eben Alexander's book Proof of Heaven and researching him, I discovered the Eternea website, leading me to Mark Ireland's wonderful book, Soul Shift. In that book, Mark talks about Helping Parents Heal, the support group co-founded by Elizabeth Boisson and Mark. After reading his book, I reached out to Mark and then to Elizabeth Boisson, and my journey with HPH began. Elizabeth befriended me as she does with everyone she meets. With her encouragement, I started a chapter of HPH in South Carolina soon after moving here from New Jersey. It is a beautiful organization that is different from other support groups because, as is expressed in our Mission Statement, "We go a step beyond other support groups by allowing the open discussion of spiritual experiences and evidence for The Afterlife in a non-dogmatic way."

I was fortunate to have a reading with Suzanne Giesemann on December 31, 2014, which completely changed my life and shifted my grief journey. I now know that when you have a reading with a medium, you should not ask for a specific word or piece of information and have that be your proof of spirit contact, but I did not know that then, nor did it matter on that day! After my reading with George Anderson, I always carried my autographed copy of his book Walking in The Garden of Souls with me; I called it my bible.

I asked Carly to mention that book, which I was holding during our reading.

During the reading, Suzanne said that she got a picture of a bible that turned into another book, and she asked me if I had a signed bible. She said the book was signed on both the left and right sides, which is unusual. Yes, it was! George had written about Carly in the hereafter on the left page and wrote The Lord's Prayer in Latin on the right page. Wow! I felt as if Carly was sitting on the couch with me as I received validation after validation. To this day, I listen with wonder at the recording of that reading.

I am honored to be a part of Suzanne's book Still Right Here, which tells the story of four HPH couples who travel together in The British Virgins Islands on a catamaran. I met Elizabeth Boisson and her husband Cyril, and Jeff and Lynn Hollahan for the first time on that boat trip. We became fast friends along with Ty and Suzanne Giesemann and experienced a magical trip together that sealed our friendships. We are all very close, and I treasure my friendship with these fellow Shining Light Parents with all of my heart.

The readings by George Anderson, Suzanne Giesemann, and other mediums have truly changed my life. I am eternally grateful for the connections made in them, which prove that our loved ones never die; only their bodies do. I continue to be amazed by the signs that Carly sends me and keep a journal of the magic to look back on when I need a reminder that she is with me always. Hearing our song "Somewhere Over the Rainbow" performed by the Hawaiian singer Iz always lets me know that Carly is close. A penny with her birth year has magically appeared four times, one I found on my birthday a few years ago. I thank her when I receive these heavenly gifts and pray they will continue.

I have met so many wonderful parents on this journey and feel blessed by the collateral beauty in my life since my daughter's transition.

My involvement with HPH is now a full-time volunteer job that I absolutely love. I spend my days talking with Elizabeth (multiple times), planning events, helping moderate a Facebook group of over 18,000 members (growing daily), reaching out to parents as a Caring Listener, planning our next conference, and participating in our almost nightly Zoom meetings.

I tell parents that I connect with that it is possible to become a "Shining Light Parent" and no longer be considered bereaved, a term I dislike. Every morning when I put my feet on the floor after waking, I recite the following "I hope that I can do something today that will honor Carly, and I pray I can help a parent who is also on this journey."

I know with absolute certainty and speak with conviction when I say that death means nothing more than the loss of one's physical body, and the love we have for our children and loved ones in spirit is eternal. Love never dies.

I believe with all of my heart that when the day comes that I close my eyes on this side of life and open them on the other, Carly will be there waiting for me. I will be ready for an adventure with her.

-Written by Carly's Shining Light Mom and Helping Parents Heal Vice President, Conference Chair, HPH Hilton Head /Bluffton Affiliate Leader, and HPH Caring Listener, Irene Vouvalides

Quinton Stone Jackson

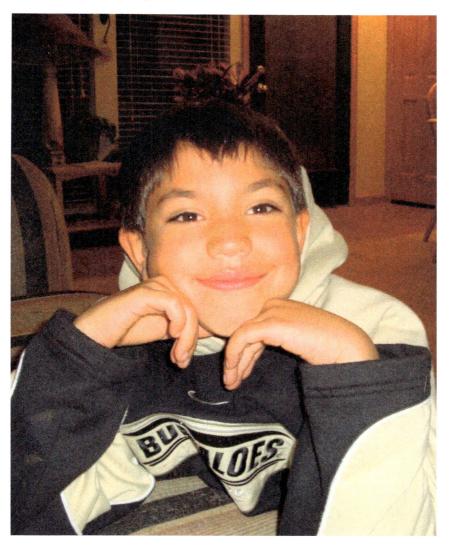

Quinton Stone Jackson was born right on time, December 15, 1999. He was unexpected as we were told we would not have any more children after our first, Cheyanne, was born in 1993. So, when Kristine wasn't feeling well in March, we thought it was the flu, and when we went to the doctor, we were shocked to discover she was pregnant. That whole exchange was a bit humorous as the doc came out and hesitantly delivered the news. Kristine's pregnancy was the unexpected part. The 'right on time' part refers to something a bit different.

Kristine and I met in Arizona and were married in 1992. From there, we started our family while living close to hers. Cheyanne was born in May 1993, generating a feeling in me I don't recall ever having experienced, that of unconditional love; I vividly remember holding her for the first time and knowing I would do anything for her. Those years were magical for me as a family and as a professional running the family business, but my heart longed for the high foothills of Colorado, where I grew up. After selling the company, I uprooted our family, taking Kristine away from her mom and Dad, and Cheyanne away from her grandparents. Doing so wasn't easy for either of them. Enter Quinton, right on time.

I worked hard providing for our family, and while the neighbors in the mountain community of Conifer embraced Kristine and me, it was still a struggle for her to be so far away from her immediate and extended family; Quinton's arrival changed that. Just as I vividly remember Cheyanne being born six and one-half years earlier, I remember the magic of Quinton being born, with his little head full of dark hair.

Quinton was heaven sent in more ways than one. Like Cheyanne, he was not a fussy baby. Given that I was off working from dawn until sunset, it was Quinton who was there for Kristine. He was there for me too when I came home; having a daughter first got me into the groove of cuddling, not something we did much of in my family, so when Quinton was born, I cuddled with him too.

As we settled into a routine, Quinton was always with Kristine. I would head out before anybody was awake, Kristine would get Cheyanne to school, and then it would just be Q and Kristine until Cheyanne returned. While it is a given that all parents have a special bond with their children, especially all mothers, the bond between Quinton and Kristine was especially deep. After twenty-nine years of marriage, I can testify just how special a woman Kristine is, and Quinton has taken that gift to a whole different level.

Most of us have heard the terms "old soul" or "old eyes." We steadfastly believe this is the result of having lived numerous lives. This term describes Quinton and his enduring presence in our lives. His vibe and energy are calm and soft, comforting not only to Kristine, but also to our daughter and me. Cheyanne and Quinton would sometimes have disagreements since they were 6½ years apart. However, if we were out for a date night and Cheyanne was left in charge, Quinton was the one who took care of her. And while I was frequently absent and tortured by my work routine, Quinton was there for me too. I can remember at one point being under the gun to get a project done. I was at my computer at 3:00 a.m. when Quinton, after using the bathroom, peeked down the stairs at me and asked, "Are you ok, Dad?" On another occasion, after a long day at the office left me tired and frustrated, I sat alone downstairs watching Star Trek – The Next Generation. I was content to be alone, not wanting to share my less-than-pleasant vibe with the rest of the family, but Quinton wasn't having it. He came downstairs, and we sat together. His presence soothed the souls of all of us.

As the years passed, we settled into a routine. Kristine held the family together; the kids went to school, and I worked hard to create the existence I wanted for my family in the high foothills along the Front Range of Colorado. Not long after Quinton started school, Kristine began to work. Kristine remembers fondly coming home from work in the evening, and Quinton always excitedly meeting her at the top of the stairs of our raised ranch as she entered from the basement. In hindsight, we learned that Quinton's loving and supportive presence went beyond what we experienced firsthand. His teachers and friends would later share many of his selfless acts, like standing up to a bully who was tormenting another on the school bus, and the hugs he would unexpectedly give his teacher on the first day of a new school year.

Another routine we enjoyed was our once-a-year, one-week vacations. We always went to Rocky Point, Mexico, also known as Puerto Penasco. These vacations were sacred because they truly were the one week out of the year when I completely relaxed and connected with my family. In 2009, the weeks leading up to our annual trip felt different. I *felt* a change coming, which was odd, given that I typically didn't have any sort of intuition. The feeling was so strong that I acted on it by slowly, over the course of a month, cleaning out my office in the building I managed. I didn't plan on going anywhere but felt I had to act in accordance with this unexpected intuitive feeling.

Additionally, the swine flu and turmoil in Mexico had reached Rocky Point, resulting in at least one death. Our extended family responded pretty forcefully and told us, "You can't go to Rocky Point this year. If you do, you could end up dead." I was incredulous! I don't respond well to being told what to do or not do, and I threatened to go alone: damn it, I needed my vacation. I will never forget the look in Kristine's eyes as I made that empty threat; she saw right through me. Ultimately, we changed our plans to avoid the possibility of a serious or potentially fatal illness.

Instead of going to Rocky Point, Cheyanne suggested we go to Lake Powell in Page, Arizona; however, everybody's intuition was pinging by now. We borrowed our good friend's two Jet Skis and trailer and headed south from Conifer. The trip was challenging because we had to go slower due to the trailer, and along the way ended up with two flat tires, but we eventually made it. We arrived mid-afternoon, unloaded our provisions from the Suburban, and loaded them onto the rented houseboat. After a quick tutorial, we headed out to the nearest shore and anchored for the rest of the afternoon and evening. We were all exhausted but beyond happy to have finally reached our destination. Once on the water, my nagging feeling seemed to have diminished, but Quinton still seemed to be acting differently somehow.

We were on the lake for the better part of a week. We fished, explored, hiked, and simply relaxed. For reasons she didn't understand at the time, Kristine packed all of Quinton's favorite foods and a case of root beer, when usually we didn't serve soda. We cruised around on the Jet Skis, but Quinton was nervous; oddly, he seemed afraid to go too fast. Additionally, he refused to go down the houseboat slide into the lake; it was as if he was scared of the impact with the water. We all enjoyed ourselves on the lake, but still, we noticed Quinton spent an excessive amount of time just staring off into the distance. Somehow, he knew something was going to happen. The day before we left the lake, I had an unusual dream.

The dream was more of a vision, unusual in its vividness and clarity, and in the vision, Quinton died. I snapped awake and felt compelled to tell both Quinton and Kristine about the dream. Quinton replied with a gravity unusual for his nine and a half years, "Dad, it wouldn't happen like that because I would just swim away." That simple statement and the way he said it was about to take on greater significance.

The day came to go home. I was all prepared and in control. Or at least at that point, I was still immersed in the illusion of having control. We had new tires on the trailer and two new spares. Still though, something was wrong with the trailer, causing the tires to rub on the trailer's wheel wells. Just past the Four Corners monument on Highway 160, we pulled off to recheck, and the trailer's axle broke. In truth, I was happy at this turn of events. We were finished with this trailer that, in my mind, had been slowing us down. I started removing a few items from the trailer and putting them inside the Suburban while Kristine called AAA to arrange for someone to haul the trailer to Cortez. As this was going on, that momentous change I had felt coming and that had made us all nervous suddenly arrived, in the form of a young lady who had fallen asleep at the wheel.

Quinton was between the back of our Suburban and the front of the still-hitched Jet Ski trailer when she came up behind us. She had veered off the road into the pullout where we were parked thirty feet away, airborne and bouncing. She hit me, sideswiped the Suburban, and then ran over the top of Kristine. Quinton was violently tossed back and forth between the back of the Suburban and the trailer. He transitioned immediately.

Our world as we knew it had come crashing down but was soon replaced with something new and wholly unexpected. Quinton immediately began sending us signs, some we noticed, and I am sure, some we didn't. Thirty or so hours after the accident, when I was finally able to fall asleep, just as I was losing consciousness, I felt my left hand being held. I thought it was so odd and tried to make sense of it. I was alone in a room, and my hand was being held. I had no previous knowledge of death or signs; I was a blank slate trying to process what I was experiencing. At that moment, all I could come up with was, "This must be the manifestation of all the prayers coming our way," but the prayers were just beginning. Weeks later, I understood it was Quinton holding my hand. Why, you ask? Because Quinton has the softest hands, something we were all intimately familiar with from routinely walking hand in hand with him. He knew; eventually, even I would figure it out.

Five days after the accident, the idea that Quinton was still quite alive pierced my numbed consciousness. Our family and close friends had come in our time of need. On this particular morning, after I left the lobby of the Marriott Courtyard in Farmington, New Mexico, and was on my way back to the hospital where Kristine had recently been moved from ICU to her own room, a medicine man in full gear approached one of our friends. He clasped her hands and said, "I have just finished performing a ceremony and was sent here to find you. The little boy wants you to know he is fine, and Tom is helping him with his transition". Our friend hightailed it to the hospital, where we all were gathered with Kristine. The moment she shared her experience with us, the energy changed in the room; all of us felt it. My first thought was, "Quinton is alive" and "Why didn't I know" it worked this way. This was my big, gigantic epiphany! Quinton was just getting started with the signs.

We arrived home to our new reality. I remember walking past Quinton's room, looking in and expecting to see him there, but he wasn't. Our friends wrapped us with their loving attention and were with us almost every step of the way. A day after Quinton's service, those friends had a tree-planting ceremony in the front yard of our home to celebrate Quinton. They planted a nine-foot-tall Blue Spruce to commemorate Quinton's nine years in physical form. During the ceremony, a hummingbird hovered directly over the tree *the entire time.* Nearly everyone saw it and understood its meaning; Quinton was there too! That whole summer, the hummingbirds acted in ways they *never had before.* One afternoon a hummingbird flew up and hovered within a foot of Kristine's face as she stood outside. On another day, one tried to fly through the window to get inside. All summer, this behavior continued and occasionally, after twelve years, still does. Another odd thing that happened, *odd in that it had never happened before*, is a small deer began bedding down and sleeping under our bedroom window. While some may consider this a coincidence, we knew otherwise.

The signs continued. Approximately six weeks after the accident, as I awoke early and walked down the hallway past Quinton's room, I heard him call out, "Dad"! I heard him, and I was awake but couldn't think fast enough to reply. About eight weeks after Quinton transitioned, I actually saw him in his room. I had just finished taking a shower in the bathroom across the hall from his bedroom. As the fogged mirror cleared, while I was cleaning my ear, which had recently been pierced so I could wear one of his earrings, I saw his reflection in the mirror as he walked across his room. Somehow he seemed taller. One of the most impactful signs was the dream visit I experienced four months after his transition.

I woke early to go to the gym. Grieving is essential, and we all grieve differently – and that is ok. I spent a lot of time in the gym working through some of my heavier emotions. On this particular morning, I turned the alarm off and went back to sleep. Immediately I found myself on the east side of our home, where we already had a sanctuary for my father-in-law, who had transitioned six years prior. As I stood there, at my feet were shadows of the deck rails and a hooded figure. I knew immediately that hooded figure was Quinton but thought I would not be able to see him when I turned around. I was wrong. When I turned around and looked up, I not only saw him for the first time since the accident, but was also able to make out the expressions on his face. He looked a bit surprised that I could see him. I, on the other hand, quickly began to freak out, thinking the whole accident had been a dream because there he was. I started calling out his name. I called three times, and each time, I grew closer to consciousness. As I called his name the 3rd time, he threw off his robe, climbed the deck rails, and jumped into my arms. As I awoke, I felt myself catching him.. The best description of my feeling as I held our son is one of incredible peace.

Kristine had signs from Quinton as well, in addition to the hummingbirds. Without going into a lot of detail, Kristine had a tough go. The accident left her with many injuries and a lot of pain, physical pain that she lives with to this day. Initially, she was on prescribed painkillers that muted her ability to connect. Once she was able to wean herself off the pain meds, Quinton came to her one night as she slept. On this particular night, Kristine had gone to sleep with her earrings on, which she rarely does. While sleeping, she saw Quinton! He came to her and said, "Mom, you don't have to be in pain anymore," and took off her earrings. When she awoke in the morning, she found her earrings neatly placed on the pillow adjacent to her. This was an incredible event in a long list of many signs.

These signs changed us, to put it bluntly. Some consider such signs silver linings and others a kind of collateral beauty. Kristine and I now know there is no death, and we know it beyond a doubt! With this knowledge, we view our time here in a different way. We know we are meant to share our experiences to help others. Between Kristine and me, we have spoken with dozens, perhaps hundreds of people over the years. We share our experiences and Quinton's signs so that others may be able to recognize the signs they've received. Once I shared with a woman I knew from work how Quinton held my hand after he transitioned, and she smiled and thanked me. She continued, sharing how when she was twelve, her mom transitioned and came one night to hold her hands, but sadly she was told by others her experience wasn't "real." After hearing me, she now knew it really did happen! This is the power of sharing and listening when we come upon someone who needs a shoulder upon which to rest.

Knowing now because of Quinton that I am also eternal, I look at my own struggles differently. Before, I would think, "Why does this keep happening to me?" But now I realize my cycles continue because I haven't learned the specific lessons I set out for myself. This simple realization helps me to continue and keep trying.

Quinton's transition and subsequent visits have made me want to tell everyone to shout it from the mountaintops. Initially, I literally told everybody, and then at the request of those close to me, we wrote *Quinton's Messages*, followed by *Quinton's Legacy*. Kristine and I live to honor Quinton and serve; in doing so, we connected with Helping Parents Heal to help others on this journey.

-Written by Quinton's Shining Light Dad and Helping Parents Heal Board Member, HPH Peoria Affiliate Leader, HPH Presenter and HPH Newsletter Columnist, Ernie Jackson, and Quinton's Shining Light Mom and HPH Peoria Affiliate Leader, Kristine

Griffin Clyde Olsen

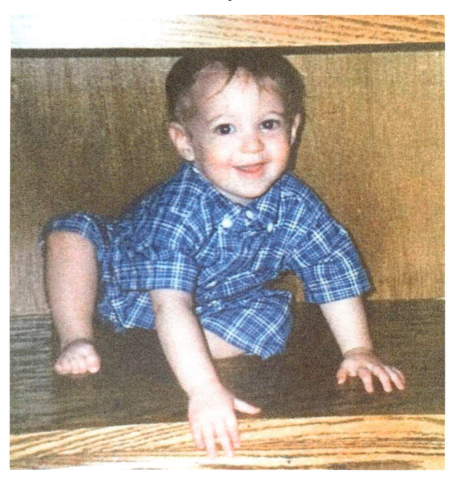

Even though Griffin was only a toddler when he transitioned, he had already demonstrated an endearing personality. He was fun-loving and mischievous. always into everything, curious, adventurous, and yet so loving. When he got in trouble for being into things, he knew that he had misbehaved. He would come to me with hugs and love knowing how I would melt. He was Daddy's Boy. He would rush to the top of the stairs when he heard the garage door lifting as I returned home from work and wait there to greet me.

Griffin was too young to ever indicate a feeling he might transition soon, but he often woke up crying late at night and would only calm down when I got up to play and spend time with him. I think he knew at some level, and this was his way of spending as much quality time with us as possible.

One particular night as I was up with him, I looked out the window to see a huge great horned owl sitting on the railing of the deck at the back of the house. It startled me at first, especially as the owl was not looking out over the valley, with his back to the house, but was staring right through the large window of the house with those giant yellow eyes.

I held Griffin as we both simply gazed at this magnificent animal. A feeling of calm came over me and I felt nothing but adoration for the owl's magnificence.

The accident happened that same month, only a few weeks after this incident. Only in hindsight have I wondered if the owl was some kind of messenger, sign, or premonition.

Griffin left this world along with his mother, Tamara, in a family car accident which also took my life in a unique and strange way. My injuries were so severe that I left my body and had a profound Near-Death Experience, wherein I joined my wife in a place of brilliant light. However, I was sent back by Tamara to raise our surviving son Spencer, who was also in the accident but not seriously injured.

Griffin was thrown from the car when his car seat broke apart during the horrible rollover wreck. I was haunted by this notion of his violent passing until I was able to encounter him, beautiful, alive, and well in those higher realms during multiple Near-Death Experiences over my 5 long months in the hospital, as I underwent eighteen surgeries due to my many life-threatening injuries.

Although we lost half our family in this horrible crash, I have had many wondrous signs from them. Griffin has sent me feathers, coins, messages, and dreams. However, one of the most powerful 'signs' came to me years after the accident.

I was asked to participate in a graduation ceremony at the local high school where Tamara had taught. So many years had passed since our tragedy that the administration had changed and much of the faculty as well. In fact, I was asked to speak completely independent of my relationship with Tamara. I was approached by a current student government member who simply knew me as part of the community, without ever having known Tamara, or the details of our story. Of course, I graciously agreed to take part and felt honored to be asked. I loved working with young people, and when they extended an invitation, I usually made it a priority to accept.

I prepared my remarks in a loose outline format and intended to speak about taking life on with gusto, learning from adversity, and choosing joy whenever possible. I arrived at the high school early. It had been several years since I had been there. The hallways were empty. I could hear my dress shoes clicking on the hard surface of the floor, accentuating my unique gait from the prosthetic. The school had been renovated in many areas, but much of it was exactly the same as I remembered from when Tamara taught there. As I made my way down the long hallway, I noticed the familiar smell of janitorial cleaning supplies mixed with the thousands of dreams and ambitions of young spirits. There was a particular part of the high school I wanted to visit. I hoped it was still very much the same, too.

At the time of the accident, when Tamara was teaching there, our little boys were in the high school daycare assistance program. Tamara and others had set up a system where teachers with young children could bring their youngsters to school. A course on early childhood development was instituted, with two qualified teachers overseeing the class. Students could make it part of their daily class schedule to come in and work with the little ones. It was a fantastic success. Our boys loved it. Spencer was old enough to tell us at the time how much fun it was, as he got a different student assigned to work with him every hour. Every fifty minutes he got to read, play, talk, and learn with a new high school aged buddy. For a young, active, and busy boy this was a dream come true. Griffin loved it too. He was cuddled and played with by enthusiastic teens all day while his mom taught in her classroom just a few steps away. When the little ones cried and fussed, this was also a great education for the high schoolers, giving them a taste of what real parenting might be like while being supervised on how to deal with the challenges parents face. As part of the course, the high school designated a small, unused atrium as a playground for the daycare kids. It provided a safe, confined place to get fresh air and play outside during the day. When the accident happened, and we lost Tamara and Griffin, the students were obviously devastated, especially those who had spent time with Griffin in the daycare.

The faculty and administration decided to dedicate this little playground to the memory of our son and call it "Griffin's Playground." They arranged a dedication and even waited until I was well enough to attend and say a few words. I was touched by their kindness and moved that there would always be a place dedicated to the memory of my little boy. Even as Spencer grew up and entered high school, the playground was still there. In fact, Spencer, as his Eagle Scout Project, updated the playground, replanted bushes, and flowers, and installed a beautiful bench with Griffin's name on it.

That was where I was going before my speech. I hadn't been to Griffin's Playground in years, and I wanted to see it. "I found it much as it had always been, but better. As I peered through the glass windows surrounding the playground. I could see that the flowers and bushes Spencer had planted had filled in and the bench was still there. To my surprise, the door was unlocked, and I was able to walk into the atrium and sit on the bench. So many years had gone by since the accident. So much had happened. I began counting dates and realized it had been seventeen years.

Then it hit me, something I was ashamed to admit that I hadn't realized until that moment: I had approached this event as simply giving a motivational speech at the local high school, until I found myself seated in that sacred little playground, on that blessed bench. Waves of emotion overcame me. Tears welled up in my eyes. This would have been Griffin's graduating class. This would have been his graduation day, had the accident not taken him so young, so many years ago.

I began to sob uncontrollably, sitting on that bench all alone. At first, I was overcome with shame for not realizing this truth until that very moment. My shame turned to gratitude when I realized that the kindness of the universe had placed me here to be a part of the celebration. It was pure chance that I had been invited on this occasion to address the graduating seniors. Nobody, not even me, had put all the pieces together. And yet here I was, honoring those who would have known my son well had he been here with them. I sat there for some time, weeping at the synchronicity of it all. I had only a few minutes before I was to meet the folks backstage in the auditorium to prepare for the ceremony. I tried to dry my eyes and regain some resemblance of composure. I also realized people were beginning to fill the hallways outside the atrium. I made my way to the nearest men's room and quickly washed my face and blew my nose. I rushed as best as I could to the auditorium and found my way backstage through the crowd that was already taking their seats.

My emotions were nearly boiling over as I announced to those who needed to know that I was there and ready. I had grabbed tissues from the men's room and stuffed my pockets with them. I stepped back into the shadows again as I nearly lost it one more time, watching all those beautiful seniors entering the auditorium. I wiped my eyes and took a deep breath as my introduction was made and I stepped out onto the stage. As I reached the podium and stood under the blinding spotlights, I struggled hard not to lose it. I looked into the faces of those graduates, glancing at those beautiful eighteen-year-old seniors who would have been the teammates, the buddies, and the girlfriends of my son Griffin. What kind of young man would he have become? What role might he have played among them all? How tall would he have grown? How would he have worn his hair?

And how different would it have been for me if I was a proud parent sitting in the audience rather than a broken man, barely holding it together, having just sat in a playground named in his son's memory, a playground where Griffin had actually spent time only days before he left this world. I knew I'd never gotten over the accident, and I supposed I never would. I'd simply gotten used to it, and this was bringing memories and all the emotions to the surface again.

I'm not sure how I got through the speech, but I knew it was far different from the one I had outlined. I sent love to each and every one of those wonderful senior souls. I shared wisdom as though this was my opportunity to speak to Griffin if he was still here. And somehow, he was. I was not alone on that stage. I felt him there with me as I looked into the eyes of what would have been such a major part of his life. He gifted that to me, to be in that moment that would have been his. And yet it was his, and mine, all in the divine order and timing that only an angel could create.

My grief was as dreadful and long-lasting as any parent's who has lost a child.. Please do not think these incredible experiences ease the pain or dry all the tears. But these small miracles may be the only thing that has gotten me through. It's been almost twenty-five years at this point from the accident. I have not gotten over it, but I have gotten used to it. In many ways it is like carrying a stone in your pocket. It never goes away, but you get used to the weight. I have learned a great deal, however. I would not know what I know, nor would my heart and soul have grown the way they have, had I not experienced Griffin's passing and his continued connection to me from the other side. He teaches me and supports me in dreams and visions to this day.

At one point, not long ago, I dreamt of Griffin. It was one of those strange, lucid dreams where I couldn't truthfully say whether I was asleep or awake. I sat on the front seat of my dad's old white pickup truck. I remembered that truck in every detail. As I looked down, I realized I wore a toddler's jumpsuit, the kind with snaps along the inner legs for easy diaper access. It was red corduroy. I followed the material down my legs to see that I was wearing little white lace-up shoes. I remembered this! I never liked that jumpsuit, nor the shoes. I remembered being in the truck, being small, and wearing this clothing. I looked out the window and noticed I was in the pasture at our Wallsburg ranch. The Black Angus beef cattle were all crowding against the truck to get at the feed in the bed.

I became frightened because in my toddler mind I thought the cattle might tip the truck over or somehow get inside. I felt uneasy when suddenly the cattle scattered, and my dad jumped into the cab of the truck with me. He comforted me. It was exactly as if I was there, experiencing it all over again. I couldn't have been more than fourteen months old. Then it hit me: fourteen months old. That's the age Griffin was when I lost him in the crash, and here I was experiencing a moment from my own life when I was that same age.

Griffin! I thought in my dream as I looked out the truck window. As I did so, the truck, the cattle, and my dad all vanished, and I was suddenly my current age standing in the pasture. Immediately to the left of me was my son Griffin, except he was no longer a fourteen-month-old child. He stood before me as a full-grown twenty-something man. It was like looking in the mirror: he was so like me in features and build, but taller and more muscular. He was magnificent.

I wanted to rush to him, but his gaze stopped me. He looked directly into my eyes, and the nonverbal communication that so often takes place in my dreams began. Without using words, he communicated to me: "I wanted you to see this so that you would know I will always remember having you as my dad."

I realized Griffin had taken me back to that moment in my life and allowed me to remember it in vivid detail in order to make his point. I was literally experiencing that time is not linear, but circular. His brief life with me was as clear in eternity as those brief moments I had just re-experienced from my childhood. I comprehended with clarity that he was grateful for me being his father and himself being my son, and also his pure intention of what he wanted me to experience in the dream.

His gaze softened, and I rushed to him. I threw my arms around him and leaned my head into his strong jaw. We hugged tightly, heart-to-heart, for what felt like a few minutes. Then he did speak; his words went right into my ear. "I have a message for you, Dad," he said. My spirit leaped with joy: a message from heaven, from my son. I expected something profound and prophetic as I leaned in to listen.

"I love you, Dad. And I'm proud of you."

That was a far simpler and more powerful message than anything I could have imagined. I had struggled, loved, worked with, ached over, and experienced so much joy while raising my living sons, but I was now communing with the son I had lost, who had become a grown, powerful, magnificent man. What a perfect gift.

I awoke with my eyes still wet. Was it real, and was "dream" even the appropriate word for such an experience? It didn't matter; it was real to me, and that was all that counted. To me, the dream showed that we are always connected, no matter what side of the veil we may be on. I learned that even the little things we did as parents mattered. The moments we create are eternal, and memories are sacred and important. I learned that no matter what my shortcomings as a father might be, my love would always come through perfectly.

Helping Parents Heal came into my life through Elizabeth Veney Boisson and Carol Sanna Allen. I have been blessed by the organization and the individuals within it ever since. Having the opportunity to meet and rub shoulders with other Shining Light Parents has been a gift. We can simply hug each other and 'know that we know.' Being able to share my story and walk with those who may be much newer to the journey has been an honor. Helping Parents Heal offers a beautiful and safe place to serve each other and learn from each other. I am so grateful for this wonderful organization and the work they do.

-Written by Griffin's Shining Light Dad and Helping Parents Heal Presenter, Jeffery Olsen

Austin Jordan Alegre

My message to all the parents who have lost a child or children is *Please take one day at a time. Take good care of yourself. Our children want us to be happy, healthy, and live life! Our children are always with us. Watch for the signs and messages that your children send. It will happen-- just be patient.*

With pleasure let me brag about my son Austin "AJ" Alegre, born on May 7, 1994. My beautiful deep blue-eyed son with gorgeous wavy long hair! Austin was such a good baby. Never gave me any trouble during his whole 15 years of life. He was always active one way or another--playing his guitar and video games, riding his bike, playing soccer-- just a full-of-life child from day one. The most beautiful smile always brightened his face. And he was the most loving kid ever. When his baby sister was born, my mom brought Austin to the hospital to see Alli. The first thing he said as he touched her hand was, *she is so beautiful!!!* Austin was always hugging and kissing his family. His smile would light up an entire room. He has a loving soul!

I feel Austin was an Angel from Heaven from day one. His presence felt like the power of LOVE! Everyone could feel it--his family, his friends, and just about anyone that he came into contact with. He was funny, fun, very intelligent and a complete smartass! In a good way! You know the movie 21? It is about counting cards in Vegas. Austin, Alli and I watched it. After the movie, Austin said, "I will be right back." Less than 30 minutes later he came back to the living room and announced, "OK I know how to count cards," and he showed us. It blew my mind!

I remember when Austin was in High School, as I was driving him to school he would tell me, "I am so tired." I asked why? He said, "I had to stay up all night with a friend to make sure that she didn't harm herself." He would do that often. When he arrived at high school early, his friends would run up to him to get one of his amazing hugs that filled their heart. He would do the same thing after school before they went home. It is hard to explain, but his hugs were healing.

Austin was loved by so many and had a ton of friends. His first job was at age 15 at Safeway. They didn't hire kids until they were 16 but he talked his way into getting that job!

Austin loved music: anything from his favorite Blink 182, Sublime, Bob Marley, 303, and so much more. He was always busy with friends, skateboarding, biking, soccer, snowboarding, or skimboarding. He loved to draw, sketch, wrench on his bike, play his guitar, and do graffiti art. He was a great student, participating in gifted programs when he was younger.

When Austin was around 2 years old, and we were living in the Bay Area, he had a febrile seizure and we had to call 911. Whenever he got sick, he would run high fevers, and I always had to put him in a cool bath and watch him carefully so he wouldn't have another seizure. I was always on high alert worrying about him and the possibility of another seizure. He visited the ER a few times after that due to high fevers. He wasn't in the clear until after he was 5 years old. To say that I was a paranoid mom is an understatement with this boy!

After Austin passed away at 15, I invited all of his close friends over to my house. I asked them to tell me all about him! I told them I wanted to know everything that parents would not want to hear. I found out some interesting things that he hid well from me…. LOL. One thing that they told me was one night, when they were in 10th grade, they were all together talking about the future and what they wanted to do when they grew up. Everyone knew what they wanted to do. Austin didn't answer them. So, they said Austin??? What about you!? Austin's response was, I don't need to worry about that! At that time, they all thought that was an odd response because they knew he would be and do something amazing. But now it all made sense to them. They said he knew! He must have known he wouldn't live long enough to care. So that must be why he lived his life to the fullest every day!

In 2009 I quit my job as a Branch Manager for a Title Company with no plan for what I would do next. I was a single mom. I couldn't financially afford to not have a job! What was I thinking??? Perhaps that I knew this would be my last vacation with my son??? So, I planned a vacation with my kids and another single mom and her two sons to Rocky Point, Mexico. I remember packing in my bedroom, just sitting on my bed, not wanting to go on this trip! Who wouldn't want to go on a vacation, right!?! I guess deep down inside I knew something was going to happen.

I remember the day I took all 4 kids quadding, and how I kept praying for Austin! Not Alli, just Austin. I was saying my Our Father and Hail Marys over and over and over again! I even yelled his name really loud, saying *Austin please slow down!* He wasn't even going fast! He turned around and smiled at me! I took a picture of him smiling at me. Not even 5 minutes later, the accident happened. I ran to my son where he was lying on the sand, pleading with the other boys to tell me what happened.

To this day I still haven't gotten an answer to that question. I know it was an accident but still! I started giving Austin CPR. I sent the boys to go get help, since we were alone in the desert. I told my daughter to turn around and not look back. I remember Alli at age 11 yelling at God, *Don't take my brother from me!* with her hands raised in the air!

Austin died in my arms on that vacation in Rocky Point, Mexico. The quad had crushed his chest and ruptured his aorta. I felt numb, of course, but at the same time surprisingly strong! My little girl needed me and needed her to be a good role model for her as she grew up. I felt the power to strive and succeed in this world. Not only for my daughter but for Austin as well. Immediately after, I wasn't sure why but as time went on, I felt Austin guiding me. I could feel the strength he was sending me.

After the accident, I didn't work for 6 months. I lost my home, lost a rental home I owned, and had to file bankruptcy. Soon after that I decided to take another chance and started my own Mobile Notary Business, which I have had for almost 13 years now. Thank you, Austin! I feel mentally strong, emotionally strong, and physically strong with the help of my son. I also remarried in 2013 to an amazing man that I know without a doubt Austin sent to me.

I have had several dream visits from Austin. One day in 2009, I saw a hummingbird and I got this feeling it was my son's spirit coming to say hi. Now whenever I see a hummingbird, I say, Hi Austin. Every day I randomly look at a clock and the times displayed are either 11:11 or 1:11, which is also a sign that Austin is with me. Or I will be driving and all of a sudden, I will look at my empty passenger seat and just reach over and put my hand out to hold Austin's. Some days when I am getting ready to go to work, I hear in my head *ok let's go* and I immediately say out loud OMG AJ you are coming with me-yay!

In my old home where we lived for 5+ years, one of the lights in the bathroom would flicker. Not all the time, just once in a while. I knew that was Austin. I ride motorcycles and one day I was riding with some friends. All of a sudden, I started to see flickering sparkles falling from the sky in front of me. I didn't know if it was my vision or what. I suddenly realized it was Austin in front of me. So, I slowed down my motorcycle and immediately afterwards items flew out of the back of a pickup truck in front of me. If I hadn't slowed down, I would have crashed for sure.

I have had a few dream visits. In my favorite, I was in a school bus, sitting on the left side towards the back. There was a boy in front of me with his hat on backwards (AJ always wore his hat backwards) and long, light brown hair. I was thinking to myself, *Oh my God this looks so much like AJ from the back.* Then I got this feeling inside me. I said Austin!!! If this is you, turn around and smile at your Mommy! Austin turned around immediately and smiled at me! I woke up right after that.

So many of his friends have had visits from Austin. My friends who knew him, see a hummingbird and they will tell me, *Austin came to visit me today.* Many in our family have had signs! His father had a dream visit where Austin spoke to him sternly. His dad hasn't dealt with Austin's passing very well. Austin told his dad, *I am here, don't look away, it is me! Please believe that I am here!* His grandma would always tell me that when she slept, she could feel him there and he would always tug at her feet. One other dream visit I had with AJ was when I got to hold him. I mean actually feel him! I spoke to him, and he spoke back, telling me how much he loves me. How much he misses me. How he is always here watching over Alli and me. The dream visits have not returned in a long, long time but our conversations are clear as day and I know he is here with me. I can feel him here. Sometimes I can hear him laughing at me if I do something silly. When I ride my motorcycle, I can feel him with me.

I have always known that there is life after death, through my grandma's teachings. I grew up Catholic but also Spiritual. My Grandma had a gift and would receive messages from her guides. I was very young, but I remember waking up and seeing my grandma in a trance of some sort and my mom transcribing her messages. So yes, even before Austin passed away, I believed. I like to get readings from different mediums. Some readings are wonderful and some just ok. I know this is because Austin connects better with some mediums than with others. I know with all my heart and soul that this is not the end! We continue in the Afterlife. My mom, my best friend, just passed, and all I can think of is OMG she is having such a reunion with her grandson. Knowing there is so much more than this life, I live my life to the fullest every day. All of my friends and family can attest to that!

In 2009 during the Christmas Holiday, my mom, my daughter, and myself were at Hansen's Mortuary here in Arizona. We were honoring all who had passed that year and we all placed an ornament on the tree. Elizabeth Boisson's daughters knew my son, since they all went to the same high school. Once the celebration ended, Elizabeth came up to me and introduced herself. We spoke for a while, and she told me her plan was to help all of us parents/grandparents with children who have passed. She asked me what my beliefs were, and I said I am spiritual but brought up Catholic. The smile on Elizabeth's face was brilliant with love. She was so excited to know that other people shared her belief in the Afterlife. HPH hadn't come to fruition yet, but Elizabeth made it happen soon after and it has been the most amazing healing component in my journey.

Attending the HPH monthly meetings, I have found so many new friends. They have truly become family to me. Ironically, several of our children who have passed all connected one way or another during their time on Earth, either from the same High School or through sports. Interesting, right?! My story is our story and Austin's mission here on Earth was to help and to teach. I am his messenger. Love to all!

-Written by Austin's Shining Light Mom, Kim Camacho

Derrick Dean Courtney

This is my story about a mother's love for her son. It's been said there is nothing like it, well except God's love for our children.

Derrick was and is my firstborn child. I have him to thank for making me a mom. An unbreakable bond that defined the foundation of our family surrounded him. Derrick knew only love, joy, happiness, and laughter in his young life.

We lived in a unique neighborhood, the kind that fairy tales are made of. The kids in the "hood" did everything together. Swimming, riding bikes, skateboard jumps, Nintendo, baseball, football, soccer, snowboarding, cliff jumping, riding quads, catching frogs, it was the best.

Derrick was always the one who included every kid. No one left out! When there was someone that got teased or left out, Derrick invited him/her into his life and those kids stuck with him and were with him though the darkest years of his life.

Derrick has a brother and sister that he was fiercely protective of. He took pride in being a role model for them and wanted them to be proud of him. We attended church regularly, and I know all 3 of them knew that the core values and beliefs learned there were the backbone of our faith and ended up holding our family together when he got sick.

Derrick was so beautiful, the pretty boy as he was called! He had a giant physique but such a gentle soul. He was so popular. There were so many friends that wanted to be around him all the time. Gee, I needed a calendar for all his social activities: sports, driving, girls, parties, working out.

He was expected to work as well during high school. He taught swim lessons with me at our school. Who knew that those would be some of the greatest times I shared with him? Derrick was so happy. He would hug me often and tell me how much he loved me.

Then this kid with a perfect life started not feeling so perfect or normal. I knew as his mom something wasn't adding up. Derrick kept reassuring me these "episodes" he was having were a result of his strict diet and training. He was a gifted athlete, and although he continued to train and work out constantly, the symptoms became alarming.

He tried to push them aside because he wanted to accomplish his goals for his future, but finally acknowledged that something was terribly wrong.

In 2004 our family changed forever. Derrick was diagnosed with Myasthenia Gravis, a rare neuromuscular form of Muscular Dystrophy. I often say the son we raised died that day, and an imposter filled in for the next decade of his life. The following years were consumed with drug treatments, blood infusions, surgeries, blood clots, therapies, addiction to pain pills and countless hospitalizations. It took a toll on him mentally, physically, and spiritually.

Derrick spent his days and nights alone in isolation from family and friends. His refuge was his bedroom. The TV was on 24/7 and was a constant companion. He was embarrassed and ashamed by his appearance, a body that had let him down. He lost most of his teeth and suffered drastic weight increases and decreases. His eyes couldn't focus, he lost the ability at times to be able to swallow, eat and speak. Literally days would go by when he didn't have the strength to get out of bed.

Derrick felt judged and misunderstood. He got frustrated at us when we couldn't understand what he was saying but was desperate to be heard. His despair and anguish only grew and increased his difficulty coping with life. He said no one understood how he felt. He was right, we didn't. I begged him to go to counseling. He refused, saying no one knew him better than I did. It ended up it was the best gift of all, more time with my sweet Derrick!

He told me often he would go before me. I said to stop talking like that. But tucked away deep in the back of my mind, I thought he might be right. Derrick knew all along that was to be.

In the early morning hours of April 25th, he knew something was happening and got out of bed and crawled to his door. We know he was trying to get to us. But the Lord said to him," I am sending an angel ahead of you to guard you along the way and bring you to the place I have prepared". Everything that could be done for Derrick on earth had been done and God knew it was time to take him home. I knew before finding him he had died. He left this place only to find love, joy, happiness, and complete serenity in his eternal home.

In her book *You are the Mother of all Mothers*, Angela Miller writes, "As a mom, sometimes it's your own inner voice that shoves you into the darkest corner of despair, like an abuser telling you over and over again you failed as a mother. Convincing you *if only* this and *what if* that, it never would have happened". Saying you coulda, shoulda done this or that so your child would have not died. I'm here to tell you that it is just not the case! *I did not fail at anything!*

I was chosen to be Derrick's mama. Yes—*Chosen*. His soul plan was long established before his physical birth and death. God put him in my world because no one could parent my son better than me! His illness and ultimate death have made me a better person.

Don't get me wrong. I was devastated and overwhelmed with grief. I thought I had a personal "in" with God and believed he would be healed. Well, God's miracle wasn't mine at all. Derrick and God knew what was going on. They just decided not to inform me of this.

92

But then, a gift from across the veil came. Derrick came to see me several days after he transitioned.

I felt like he was RIGHT THERE! He told me of the plans he had for us. We would start a nonprofit charity, called The Healing Cross Project, as a grassroots effort to spread understanding about human suffering. The message would be spread by the distribution of the healing cross that "YOU ARE NEVER ALONE". Derrick even went so far as to tell me who would help me on this endeavor.

At Derrick's funeral, I spoke of my dream visit. Our friend KNEW he was the one chosen by our son to make it a reality, and he readily agreed to get involved.

Shortly after, I had a group reading with the highly acclaimed medium, Susanne Wilson, the Carefree Medium. I was one of about 20 people in the room. Derrick monopolized every conversation and butted in so I could be informed of every detail about our nonprofit. He got his point across and today the project has grown beyond my wildest dreams.

It ends up that this journey saved me from not giving up and taught me to persevere. It taught me to fight the undeniable path of separation from my child and a fight for my own survival.
Several weeks after Derrick died, a client of mine who had heard of Derrick's passing called me. She wanted me to meet someone who had started a group for parents who had lost a child.

I reluctantly went, and on that fateful day I met Elizabeth Boisson, co-founder of Helping Parents Heal. I knew I was in good company for the 2 of them were wearing makeup, had their hair done, and were dressed to the nines. I looked like something that the cat dragged in.

I said to them, "I'll have what you're having!" It was at that moment I knew I was going to be ok. That someday I would once again put makeup on, wear fabulous clothes, and even leave the house! I would learn that time really does heal, and that laughing and smiling would return to me again.

Today, the parents from this incredible organization are my forever friends, parents I can share anything with and never be judged and be absolutely accepted just as I am! I have learned to succeed instead of giving up. We were all so happy to be chosen for Craig McMahon's documentary "Life to Afterlife, Mom, Can You Hear Me". I have learned that part of the growth is sharing my story so that others can get to where I am today. The Salvation Army's mantra is doing the most good. This I MUST do to make a difference.

I have met the most gifted Mediums in the business. Derrick contacts them occasionally when he can't seem to get through to me. I continue to have readings on occasion to stay dialed in to my son.

And I must tell you about the signs from Derrick. Different people interpret them as coincidences, validations, or synchronicities. At the beginning of my healing, I was beset by anger and grief that I either couldn't see those signs or that Derrick couldn't get through to me. I thought, what am I doing wrong? I have learned along the way that Derrick doesn't have to knock me on the head to make his presence known.

He loved rain, thunder, and a cloudy day. So, when that kind of weather happens, I feel him all around me. Or when the wind blows and the night sky seems to glow brighter, I know it's him. There have been signs that undoubtedly have been from Derrick. There have been a few, but significant nonetheless!

Recently our alarm kept going off in the middle of the night. This happened three nights in a row, so we contacted the company. They came to check the system and said it was working correctly. That very night it happened again. The panel showed that someone was in our billiard room. Derrick's dad and I went to that room to see what was going on. We both simultaneously experienced that ah-ha moment and knew it WAS DERRICK checking in.

During one reading, Derrick told Susanne Wilson that I should look out for a red balloon. I thought that was pretty funny and random. But sure enough, several days later, my grandson brought a bouquet of balloons home from school. One by one, they popped-- except for the red one! That evening I thought about that red balloon and Derrick. I didn't see any further significance until the balloon moved out of the kitchen and down a long hallway. We're talking about traveling 20 feet before turning right out of the kitchen. Then another 40 feet to the end of the hallway and turning right to enter my son's bedroom. That red balloon ended up above Derrick's bed and stayed put for another two months! He wanted to let me know he was STILL RIGHT HERE.

And one more:
My grandson Owen (who is Derrick's mini-me) was scared about riding the school bus. He reluctantly got on, hiding his tears so no one would make fun of him. But after school, he came over to let me know that everything was great. I asked what had occurred on that ride. Owen then told me that Derrick sat next to him and rode the bus with him to and from school! He proceeded to inform me that Derrick was wearing a purple dress! He thought his uncle looked hysterical. At a later reading, Derrick confirmed that yes, he was on the bus with Owen, and that the purple dress was a robe. Of course, it was purple--Derrick's favorite color.

The signs are there, ready for you to recognize and accept that your loved one is coming to check in and say how much they love you! How great is this!

I know outsiders always want to know what we're drinking as we laugh, hug, share stories and love spending time together. We say it's our kids that have brought us together, and I for one am grateful that my son still guides me through this physical life.

I know that handling grief is a process that never stops; however, it can be part of a life worth living. I can talk openly about not fearing death, and instead being excited when my ultimate moment comes and death knocks on my door, for that is when I will see my sweet Derrick once again.

This is what I know FOR SURE.....

-Written by Derrick's Shining Light Mom, and HPH Presenter, Kim Courtney

Garrett Martin Savoie

Hello to Everyone who is reading my story in this book. If you are, then you most likely have had someone close to you transition, pass to the Other Side, Go Home – so many terms for leaving us here on Earth. Thank you for reading my story, and as my Mentor, Susanne Wilson, The Carefree Medium, always says: *I hope you find it hopeful, helpful, and healing.*

My name is Laurie Martin Savoie, and I've been married to my amazing husband, Tom, since 1985. We had our first baby, Kailee Teal, in April 1990. Garrett Martin Savoie, our second child, was born August 30, 1991, 17 months after his sister. They were both born in Calgary, Alberta, Canada. As a baby, Garrett was a handful from the start, barely eating food but living on air and sunshine and not needing much sleep. In February 1998, when Garrett was 6 ½ years old, we moved to Phoenix, Arizona but Garrett was always proud to be a Canadian! He then became big brother to Chantal Karli, our USA baby, who was born on November 9, 1998.

As parents to Garrett, we had to keep that kid busy all the time. He was involved in sports like baseball and hockey. His dad Tom coached Garrett's teams for many years. When not out on the ice, Garrett would get all of the neighborhood kids playing street hockey, something he did constantly in Calgary and Phoenix!

He didn't really like going to school because he had a hard time sitting still all day long. He lived to be active! He loved going to summer sports camps, Vacation Bible School camps, and when he was 14 years old, he got a summer camp counsellor job. This led to him working during the school years at the afterschool programs for working parents. He absolutely loved those jobs and recruited several friends to work there as well. He loved kids and they loved him because he would play sports with them constantly. His employers all said that he was very respectful. As a teenager, he held several other jobs, always earning his own money to spend on paintballing and video games.

He loved visiting his family in Canada and traveling on many trips and adventures with us. He had ADHD, which led him to have little fear or awareness of any consequences to his actions, so he lived fearlessly. He was quite shy but had a great sense of humor. He constantly had us laughing. He had a tender, loving, giving heart. He loved animals, and would help anyone in need, in any way, at any time. He loved his family, was a respectful teenager at home, and hated to disappoint us. He was known for his beautiful eyes and smile.

He had graduated high school and was in his first semester of college when things started going awry in his life. He loved history and archeology but hadn't decided what he wanted to be or do in life yet. Now I hear he is helping kids in heaven, which I believe, because that's totally him!

We will always cherish him as our beloved son, even though he was a ton of work while on Earth! He was a great brother, cousin, and nephew. His circle of friends was often at our house hanging out, and I honestly don't think he knew how many people cared for him or how he impacted them. Everyone was devastated after he took his life, and no one could believe it, as it seemed to come out of the blue, with no warning.

Garrett himself never hinted that he felt he would transition early in his life, but right after Kailee heard about her brother, she said to me: "Oh Mom, you always KNEW"!! I believe my soul knew, because the night before Garrett left us, my Mom appeared to me in Spirit, and I said to her: "You better not be here for what I think you're here for…."

He never seemed to fit on Earth. When he was born, he looked like an old man. So, I believe he was an old Soul, and the way he lived his few years on Earth, jam-packed with activity and relationships, makes me think that his own soul knew his time here would be short.

At the beginning of 2010, Garrett started doing drugs and left home and abandoned our family for six devastating months. His personality totally changed, becoming hardened and uncaring. After getting into trouble with the law that summer, he moved back home. He got clean, got a job, and was once again a loving member of our family. We got our son back for a glorious three months! Then suddenly, prior to a court date in November 2010, he took off for 10 days and didn't communicate with us. We suspect that he had relapsed, and even though I had spoken to him on the phone the night before his court date, he didn't show up. He didn't answer our calls that morning. I found out where he was staying, frantically drove over there, got the office to open his apartment door.

I found my beloved son sitting on the couch, with bare feet, and cartoons playing on the tv, but he was lifeless. I was later informed by the detectives that I had missed him by only 10 or 15 minutes. My beloved Garrett, who was never around any gun more powerful than a BB gun in his entire life, had taken his own life with a gun. I believe he was scared of going to jail, but I won't know this for sure until I see him in Heaven. He left no note and had never spoken about taking his life at all. So of course, many shoulda, woulda, coulda questions came, not to mention, total disbelief and shock.

I was fortunate to be surrounded from the very beginning by loving and concerned friends, family, coworkers, and community. These wonderful people planned everything, cleaned our house, visited in the first few days and continued for many months to check on us. They did absolutely everything, even cooking for us for the next 8 months! They also brought us a treasured Angel Tree, which the community filled with 200 ornaments in remembrance of Garrett. To this day, I can honestly say that I haven't lost any friends, only gained many more.

The most valuable tool I felt that worked for me was my decision not to let this take me down to the carpet. I read books and started back on my spiritual path, seeing mediums, and then strengthening my own gifts, as I was already communicating with my Mom and Garrett.

When I was filming the Helping Parents Heal "Life to Afterlife" documentary with Craig McMahon, he asked me "Are you talking to Garrett while we are doing this?" My reply: "Why yes, I am listening to him!" Which, in a roundabout way, is how Garrett helped with the title: "Life to Afterlife, Mom Can You Hear Me?" Pretty cool.

I can't narrow down just one sign that we received from Garrett, because we had so many right away. The first was a double rainbow after his Celebration of Life ceremony.

A medium that Garrett found on Earth from Heaven - April Farrall. He proceeded to give her 45 minutes of clear, concise messages that she relayed to my aunt, who was her friend. April then called me three days later with 3 ½ hours of so many more validations, explanations, and messages that firmly reflected Garrett's personality and proved his continuing existence. This changed and shaped our families' early grief and gave us hope that we could survive this tragedy. I now knew without a doubt that Garrett was safe and at peace in Heaven. He informed us that his transition by suicide was no big deal, as if he simply stepped from one room into another with no judgment from anyone. That was a big healing piece for me.

On Christmas Day I asked Garrett for a BIG sign from Heaven to show that he was with us. All 4 of us came through the garage door into the hallway, after going to friends for dinner that night, to discover that one of our many family photographs that was hung up high, so no one could have brushed against it, had fallen off the wall and smashed onto the floor, shattering the glass. A BIG Sign with a BIG mess to clean, but I didn't care – I KNEW it was him.

In February 2011, a couple of months after Garrett transitioned, a red balloon offered further signs. There is NO doubt in anyone's mind that Garrett followed our directions, moving a balloon in our house, and doing what we asked the "Garrett balloon" to do. Garrett's non believing cousin, Eric, said to the balloon: "Ok, if you really are Garrett, go get me a beer please." The "Garrett balloon" then floated out of the kitchen, about 3 feet off the floor, through doorways, turning corners, going down a long hallway and into the laundry room where it stuck itself to the drink fridge!! We all followed this balloon with our mouths hanging open, not one of us thinking to grab our phone and record this incredible act from Spirit. Eric cheered Garrett in Heaven with his beer from the fridge, and instantly became a Believer!

Another balloon sign occurred in Kansas with Garrett and Garrett Ziff. A bunch of us were sending up purple Memory balloons for a group we are in: HOPE ASAP. Everyone else's balloon ascended together in a pack into the sky. Our single balloon, labelled Garrett X 2, drifted in the other direction, about 3 feet off the ground, to the opposite side of the house, and wedged itself into a hedge of bushes. I looked at Michelle and said, "My Garrett never followed the rules!" She looked at me and said: "You think My Garrett did??" After about 15 minutes the balloon unwedged itself and went on its own path up into the sky. We laughed together and it was comforting to know that our two Garretts were together in Heaven, being themselves, just as they were on Earth!

As a young teenager Garrett loved to play with BB guns. We have found different colored BB's all over the place, in strange places. His sister Kailee has even found them in Hawaii. Our latest sign was finding one on the bathroom floor of our new house. It appeared overnight while we slept, where we couldn't have missed it the day before. There's no way it could have gotten there besides being sent to us from Garrett in Heaven!

One of the things I decided early in my grief journey was that I was going to surround myself with people whom I thought could help me survive this devastating event.

I saw a Spiritual Counselor to help deal with my grief and she asked me "What gifts did you receive from Garrett's passing?" I thought she was nuts ... After thinking about it, however, I realized that I had eliminated negativity from my life, small things happening were so unimportant and those books were right – Why sweat the small stuff? I had survived the funeral of my child, so I could survive anything. I have gained an entire new network of people and friends in my life, who are now like a second family. I became more spiritual than I already was, and I no longer keep my spirituality and gifts a secret; I now use them to help others heal as well.

I heard about Helping Parents Heal shortly after it began from a friend, but for whatever reason I didn't attend any meetings for several months. I eventually went to the meetings in the Spring of 2011 when they were still fairly small, led by Elizabeth and Mark in the Logos Center in Phoenix. I immediately felt like I was with people who could understand me because they were talking about the Afterlife, signs, and everything that I had been ferociously reading about and knew to be my own truth. I now consider Elizabeth, Mark, and Helping Parents Heal to be my Second Family! I am HPH Secretary, a Board Member, and a Caring Listener, so you really can see they are stuck with me!

I participated in Craig McMahon's documentaries: *Life to Afterlife: Mom, Can You Hear Me?* and *Life to Afterlife: I Want to Talk to the Dead*. I am also the author of a book to help others: *The Ripple Effect Invisible Impact of Suicide* and a story contributor in the book *Loss, Survive, Thrive: Bereaved Parents Share their Stories of Healing and Hope* by Meryl Hershey Beck.

Thank you for reading about my beloved Garrett and my journey through grief and healing. I am sending love, healing energy, and hope for a healing journey for you, too. Surround yourself with people who can help you and choose to be happy and peaceful, because that's how everyone is in Heaven, and they want us to feel the same!

-Written by Garrett's Shining Light Mom, Helping Parents Heal Board Member, HPH Secretary, Caring Listener and Presenter, Laurie Savoie

Sean Patrick McCarthy

On a chilly February day, a beautiful child entered the world, my son Sean. I remember him trying to lift his head, looking around with curiosity at the room. I could sense the wisdom in his eyes and my heart was bursting with love for him.

Sean is my only son, our second child, born 18 months after his sister Shannon. From the moment he entered this world, we had a connection that is hard to describe. As a baby, he wanted to be with me as much as possible, so I would carry him in a backpack even when I was doing housework or cooking. He was keenly aware of his surroundings, and content to chew on my hair and laugh as I carried him from place to place. He loved to travel in his backpack. Many times, I would have Shannon in a stroller and Sean on my back. He was rarely fussy as long as he was close to me. I felt as if we could read each other's minds, a feeling that only grew stronger as the years progressed.

Sean's personality was one of kindness and empathy. He was always supportive of those less fortunate, whether with needed cash, or sometimes just a smile. When his elementary school classmates wrote a top 10 list describing him, *kind* and *sweet* were at the top. He was humble, never boasting about his many accomplishments and he never had a problem sharing what he had with other children. Many times, he would offer them some treasured item even before they even asked.

One instance I will never forget concerning his generosity was when he and Shannon went with their aunt Kathy to New York City. He was in elementary school, and I had given both him and his sister money for toys at FAO Schwartz. By the time they got there, Sean was almost out of cash. He said he would buy whatever toy he could afford with what he had left as he had given most of his allotment to homeless people along the way. When Kathy asked why he had done so, he responded, "Because they needed it more than I did". This became his mantra for life. I vividly remember a conversation with two of his friends at his service about a time when Sean sat with them all night and talked them through a challenging period. "He saved my life," one of them told me.

He was also a gifted athlete, a member of state champion baseball teams and swimming champion leagues. He excelled at tennis, soccer, and was state champion in golf. During the summers I would take both Shannon and Sean to swim practice, after which he would rapidly change into his baseball uniform and go on to play for two teams. My days were spent driving from game to game and he loved every minute of it. He was both a pitcher and a catcher, but his favorite position was catcher. He loved the energy of being on a team and thrived in that environment. His team and coaches showed their appreciation by having a high school trophy named after him.

As he grew older, he discovered a passion for golf. Although in high school golf was a team sport, it was also a game of solitude and skill. Sean read every golf magazine he could get his hands on, worked at golf courses after school and weekends, and was selected to caddy for professional golfers. His high school coach was one of his biggest supporters. Sean loved the sport so much that he seriously considered going professional after college and was willing to do whatever it took to achieve his goal.

When he left to attend Virginia Tech, Sean entered the Corp of Cadets program, the military equivalent of a service academy. The program was rigorous and left him no time for golf. In true form, he excelled in the Corp, becoming one the highest-ranking students there. He put a tremendous amount of work into becoming a commanding officer and his cadets had great respect for him. When I would visit, they would tell me how much they enjoyed having Sean as their commander. Even though he was tough, he was fair.

During senior year at Virginia Tech, Sean decided that he wanted to make the Navy his career, following in the footsteps of his dad and grandfather. He graduated as an ensign, and we couldn't have been prouder of him. His first tour of duty was as a damage control officer, and he learned a lot about life on a destroyer in the middle of the ocean. He excelled at his job, which didn't surprise me at all. When his duty officer asked him about his long-term career plans with the Navy, Sean said he was interested in Naval Special Warfare. I remember him calling to ask my permission. My stomach knotted up. When I asked him why such a dangerous billet, he said he wanted to make sure that he could bring those under his command home safely. He was never concerned about his own safety, only about the lives of others. While on duty at sea, he was put in charge of an operation to save a sinking fishing vessel. All aboard were saved, and Sean received the Navy Achievement medal. We didn't know until he transitioned that he had been awarded not one but two Navy Achievement medals. Again, humble but courageous.

I have been asked whether Sean ever had a premonition of his passing. I don't believe he felt that he would transition early; however, I was never comfortable with the assignments he was given. The Navy sent him to places in the Middle East that he could not disclose for reasons of national security. In our numerous conversations over the years, if the subject of death came up, he would plug his ears saying, "Don't you even think of going anywhere". It wasn't that he feared death, he didn't. In fact, he gravitated towards Buddhism and their view of death as just slipping out of one dimension into another. He seemed to handle the dangerous situations he was in with grace and acceptance. When his peers transitioned we would talk about it, sometimes for hours. I know for sure that Sean never feared death for himself. We both understood that no amount of worry would affect the final outcome. However, our relationship was one in which we couldn't imagine life without the other in it. That was his greatest fear and mine.

After he returned from deployment, I felt a sense of ease that he was home in San Diego, safe from the uncertainty of the Middle East. He was excited to have received an assignment to Naval Special Warfare in Virginia Beach, VA. He drove across the country in three days, rented a beautiful apartment across the street from the beach, and began to purchase furniture for his new home. He would send me pictures to get my opinion. I remember him calling full of excitement about having a washer and dryer in his apartment. Funny how little things mean so much now. On a Thursday afternoon, he decided to check in early at base and drive around to become familiar with his new duty station before reporting the following Monday. That was the last time I heard from him.

That Friday he had planned to have friends over to watch the World Cup on his new 55-inch TV. He had stocked his refrigerator full of food and drinks. He would text me daily, and when I didn't hear from him, I thought he had lost his phone in the chaos of moving, which he had done numerous times. When we hadn't heard from him in 3 days, we had a friend of his who was a naval officer call the base to see if he was there. They said he was doing a walk around and they would give him the message to call home. Hours went by and we heard nothing. We decided to call the police for a wellness check. When they said his car was in the parking garage, my stomach dropped. I knew something was terribly wrong.

The officer said that he had been shot in his apartment and they were starting an investigation. I couldn't wrap my head around what I was hearing, because only a few hours earlier, I was told he was at the base and safe. Nothing made sense to me.

After the initial shock, my motherly instincts kicked in. Even though I had studied the survival of consciousness for years before Sean's transition, his death propelled me to find out where he was, and how to communicate with him. I would have to learn a new language, the language of spirit. Sean immediately began sending signs that he was fine and right there with us. I found a foot-long white feather in my luggage when I flew to Virginia Beach to bring him home. My sister bought a Coke from a vending machine at the hotel, and the name Sean was on the can. Of course, I missed most of the early signs because I was deep in grief and shock. I couldn't fully accept that Sean was still with us until a couple of weeks later, during a reading with an evidential medium, when she told me, "Sean wanted to wish his dad a happy birthday and he was sorry it was under those conditions". We were planning a funeral for Sean, instead of a party for his dad. He also talked about his sister moving in with her boyfriend, which I adamantly denied. I called my daughter and she said, "How did you know? We just discussed it last night". That was evidence I couldn't dismiss.

Before we hung up, the medium said, "Sean mentioned beeps, like a truck backing up, listen for them, that will be him". I just laughed because this made no sense. But immediately a truck started backing up in front of my house where they were paving the street, making that exact beeping noise. "Sean is laughing now," the medium said. I heard beeping repeatedly for months after that at the strangest times, like 3:00 am when I would go outside to meditate under the stars. Even today I will hear beeping at the most unusual times, usually between 3 and 5 am when I am out walking my dog.

I started seeing numerous shooting stars almost nightly, and my solar lights that hadn't worked in months would start flashing when I was talking to Sean. They had become so entangled with my aloe vera that I didn't want to cut my hand trying to get them out, and now they would blink and light up when I asked Sean a question. That was just the beginning.

Signs, signs, everywhere signs. That song resonates in my brain when I think of all the signs in the past 7 years. I will share something that happened recently which is nothing short of amazing.

In 2019 we were on vacation on the west coast of Florida at a condo we own. I really loved being by the water, especially the Gulf. The dolphins would swim around us in the ocean. There was something special about this area. I decided to look around for a possible future home. I found a beautiful community that I loved; however, no houses were available at the time. A couple of days later, my husband Kevin joined me, and we decided to drive around, just to become familiar with the area. As luck would have it, we stopped at this community to talk to the manager, Kate. We told her about a street we would choose if we had the option. She said, "Well, there is a house on that street that just came back on the market". We walked across the street, and immediately fell in love with the lot. The house needed a lot of work, but there was something special about it. We made an offer which was accepted the next day.

Once back in Arizona, I began to realize that I would be leaving the home that Sean loved. My stomach sank. I began to cry and asked him to please let me know if we were doing the right thing. We still had three days to rescind the contract. When I went to his room to start packing up his belongings, I heard him say, "Look in my luggage". I hadn't opened his luggage in years, it was still too painful. I reluctantly opened his suitcase and noticed what looked like a real estate brochure at the bottom on the right side. When I pulled it out and opened it up, it was the exact home we had just purchased. The agent we had spoken with had only three brochures because the house had supposedly sold a few days earlier. However, the original buyers walked away at the signing, and the listing wasn't public yet. Our agent Debbie gave us one copy, which then left only two, one for her and Kim, the selling agent. I stood there stunned, but then thought perhaps Kevin might have put it in there for some odd reason. I left the casita and went into his office asking why he had put the brochure in Sean's luggage. He gave me the strangest look and said he had no idea where Sean's luggage was. I showed him the brochure of the house (the edges were wrinkled from the luggage). He then went to his briefcase and pulled out his copy! We both stood there in silence for a moment. That was the validation I was looking for: Sean was giving a thumbs-up that he was just fine with us moving--in fact I think he found the house for us. That was all I needed to get excited about our new adventure, knowing he would be right there with us.

I went back and listened to a previous reading that had taken place over a year ago. In it, Sean mentioned swimming in the pool of our new house, overlooking the golf course, and close to the beach. At the time I didn't think much of it because no medium is 100% correct. I had never planned on moving and thought the medium might have misunderstood Sean's message. I stand corrected. This home has a pool, spa, a golf course right behind it, and is of course located by the beach.

Sean is also very present with his sister. Recently she received an email with the name Sean McCarthy on it, for a high school soccer league registration form. It showed full payment. She sent me the picture saying, "I have no idea where this came from, and how would this organization I have never heard of even get my email?" There was no way to trace it, but Sean was a soccer player, and loved the game. I told her it was just his way of saying "Hi" and letting her know he was right there with her. His 4-year-old nephew has seen Sean since he was a baby and talks about him and even showed me where he slept when he visits.

There have been numerous blessings since Sean's transition. The one I will share with you is having my own experience on the other side. On a cool Easter evening in 2015 I experienced a sudden drop in my potassium and magnesium. One minute I was here in the physical, and the next, I was standing across from my dad in spirit. I was surrounded by the most intense light and unconditional love. When I looked at my body, I was no longer a human, but a being of light. My beloved dad beamed with love, and I felt safe and home. I was told I had not completed my life mission, so I was sent back. I remember the nurse saying, "She's back". After opening my eyes, I was upset to be here again. There are no words to describe the beauty and love I experienced on the other side. However, from that moment on, I knew that Sean not only survived his physical death but is thriving in the non-physical. He guides me every day, and I feel even closer to him. Nothing separates us now. Death is an illusion, that I know for sure. We only drop our physical body, but we continue to live and grow on the other side. I now understand that death is only a change in dimensional frequency and that our loved ones are very close to our physical realm. I came back and immediately began writing a book to honor Sean, called *The Myth of Dying*.

Shortly after Sean's transition, I discovered Helping Parents Heal. I remember it well. I was having an astrology reading with Maxine Taylor. She asked me, "Have you ever heard of an organization called Helping Parents Heal? I keep hearing you need to join them." Immediately after our call ended, I contacted Elizabeth Boisson and have been so blessed with her guidance and by the amazing community that has helped me to heal. I was welcomed with open arms, and now do my best to offer healing, paying it forward. The meetings were wonderfully uplifting, and I always left with a big smile on my face. It felt like a family reunion, some of us on this journey longer than others, but as the saying goes, "We are all here to walk each other home". Helping Parents Heal has not only healed my heart, but I have made lifelong friends that I will cherish until I finally go home. I am forever grateful to Maxine for suggesting HPH, and to Elizabeth for continuing to teach everyone that our children truly are Shining Lights.

In loving memory of my son Lt. Sean P. McCarthy 1987-2014

-Written by Sean's Shining Light Mom, HPH Presenter & HPH Admin, Linda McCarthy, PhD

Garrett Nathan Ziff

My name is Michelle Ziff, mom of Garrett and his two younger brothers. I hope you can take bits and pieces of my journey to help you in yours.

On March 10th, 1989, Garrett Nathan entered this world the same way he lived in it. HIS WAY. At almost eight weeks early, he was ready to make his grand entrance. Although weighing only 4 lbs. 14 oz., and spending 10 days in the NICU, Garrett had such a strong will to survive, thrive and prepare us for our future family of five.

Garrett had big blue eyes, light brown curls, and a constant smile on his beautiful face. He was nurturing, even as a toddler. So at two, when his brother Jordan was born, and six years later, their baby brother Adam, Garrett was overjoyed. He held and kissed them constantly. He adored babies and animals, ALWAYS.

Garrett loved attention and he loved an audience. It started with performing in theatre productions at a young age, to doing and saying things that were just so funny (according to him). Eventually he became the drummer in a heavy metal band known as Age of Evil. Members of the band included his brother Jordan and another set of brothers, who happened to be their best friends. While most of them were still in High School, they were signed to a European label. It was an exciting and crazy time for them, living the lives of rock stars. While the other three were more disciplined and committed to writing and practicing, Garrett loved the "lifestyle". He didn't practice much. He would just show up to rehearsal and play his ass off. He was a gifted drummer and also played guitar and piano. Just so talented.

Of course, along with the rock star lifestyle came drug use and poor life choices. Garrett, just wanting to have fun, experimented with many different temptations, believing he was invincible. Sadly, this was not the case. Over his final five years, Garrett struggled with the monster of heroin addiction. My husband Scott and I tried everything: different kinds of treatment facilities, sober living, counselors, meetings for him, for us, boundaries, etc., until we realized there was nothing we could do. We couldn't fix it. Garrett had to do the work if he wanted to find recovery. And it was HARD work. Even while using, Garrett always held a job. His employers and coworkers all loved him. Despite his addiction, he remained a hard worker, smart, and a good friend to everyone. In addition, he was able to hide things really well. Inside he could be crumbling, but he ALWAYS had a smile on his face. In fact, his little brother Adam picked 'The Great Pretender', by Queen, to play at his funeral. It was a perfect choice.

On March 10th, 2016, his 27th birthday, while engaged to his fiancée Peyton, and after months of staying clean--or so we thought--Garrett passed away on the bathroom floor of his grandma and papa's house from an accidental heroin overdose.
I don't think Garrett had any idea he would pass at such a young age. However, as I'm writing this and thinking about how much he crammed into 27 years, maybe he DID know and wanted to experience as much as he could in those short years.

When someone you love suffers from an addiction, you are always aware, in the back of your mind, of what could ultimately happen. Knowing that, you want to make sure you tell them often how much you love them, how proud you are of them and their accomplishments, how if your love could have fixed them, they would have been fixed years ago, how you'd do ANYTHING. You would constantly hug and kiss them… you'd basically make sure they knew and felt ALL the good things from you that you wanted/needed them to.

So, in a nutshell, the five years of Garrett's addiction, while incredibly difficult for us all, were kind of a gift. We didn't take that time for granted. Garrett knew all about the deep love we felt for him. We have no guilt or regrets. In that way we're very fortunate.

I started getting signs from Garrett immediately. He would put thoughts in my head to help me. Like my first thought: "I'm so happy for Garrett that he doesn't have to struggle every day anymore", instead of feeling sad for myself. (I was very sad, but he put that on the back burner) He gave me a level of strength that I had never had in my life. I had to be okay for our other boys and for Scott. For the first six months after Garrett's passing, Scott was really struggling. I needed to be the strong one. Then we flip-flopped. Scott was able to be strong for me when it finally hit. Thank goodness our "lows" always seemed to come at different times.

Five days after Garrett passed, a family friend, who happens to be a medium, reached out. It was Scott's birthday. She had a message from Gar. "Happy birthday, Dad. Please do not be sad about my death. Please celebrate my rebirth, because I was reborn to protect you in ways that I could not protect myself. I love you." That year's birthday present was the best one Scott ever received.

I have to throw in that Garrett and I used to watch TV shows about mediums, hauntings, and the Afterlife. These topics fascinated us. Garrett knew that if there was ever a mom who would recognize signs and welcome validations, it was ME!

A couple weeks later our friend had a message from Garrett for me. "My rage was never against you; it was against myself because I was scared. Scared of being hurt, but I ended up hurting myself, and you. I always wanted to be a ghost and play tricks on people, but looking from the outside in now, the world is harsh, and I just want to help everyone. Please know that even though my soul is here now, you will always be my mother, no matter where I am or what lifetime I am living. I was able to learn to love so hard because of you. Just know that I thank you for the life you gave me in this world. Thank you for being my biggest fan." I couldn't have asked for a better message from him.

Then the friend wrote these beautiful words, from her to me. I mean, WOW! I think I was walking on clouds the rest of the day. "I will always let you know when I feel or hear anything. Feeling him let me feel the love he felt for you and his family is just phenomenal. Not often do you feel that kind of pure love."

Garrett sends me white feathers, hummingbirds, and dragonflies. A blue dragonfly specifically. I named him Blue. He's landed on my toes and fingers on two separate occasions. Multiple times on both days.

Fortunately, and unfortunately, my cousin Juliet was already a member of Helping Parents Heal after losing her son Noah. I knew how much the meetings helped her.

Eleven days after Garrett transitioned, I went to my first Helping Parents Heal meeting. Christine Salter was the guest medium. Garrett came through loud and clear. Christine looked over at me and my cousin and said: "I have a young male with crazy hair and he's all over the place". Garrett's hair was wild, and he had so much energy. He apologized for how he passed. He was so sorry that it happened at his grandparents' house. Garrett was one of those kids who didn't really know how to filter. Every medium who's given us validations has had to throw in a swear word, whether they wanted to or not. It's usually F@%*K, but in a group setting it's a less offensive word. What can I say? That's just my Gar.

He has been an excellent communicator ever since. About six months later, our intercom system started clicking whenever I came into the kitchen. It's been broken for over 25 years. It is hidden on the wall in the corner, behind my favorite piece of furniture. I got confirmation that it was Garrett when I had a reading with Susanne Wilson a few months later. The clicking lasted for about a week and then stopped.... until a few days ago.

I'm finishing up my chapter to send in. I'm already a couple days late (the story of my life) and I know Garrett is shaking his head, watching me scramble to finish up, and pushing me to get my ass in gear so it will be included in the book. I've been told by many mediums that he is so proud of me for helping other parents. He helps me from the other side with so many things. You need to make sure you ask for their help and thank them afterwards. It makes them want to help even more. They need to know that YOU know that it's them.

Garrett has pushed me to focus on the positive in everything. Some days are harder than others, but there is ALWAYS something positive to be grateful for. I feel so fortunate to have had him here on earth for 27 years. He makes his presence known in so many ways that bring me so much comfort. I wish you could hear the clicking of the broken intercom right now in the background. Susanne Wilson told me that I was going to either write a book or be in a book. So, there you go! For five years I haven't heard the intercom. Garrett is cheering me on, wanting me to share as many things with you, the reader, as I possibly can, to give you hope in finding joy and happiness again. And to understand that our kids are still with us.

I miss seeing his beautiful eyes and smile, I miss his laugh, I miss holding him, I miss his smell, and so much more. Speaking of smells, another sign from our loved ones is the scent that's reminiscent of when they were here. It can be perfume, the smell of their house, anything that reminds us of them. I smell cigarettes when my Garrett is around. In places where nobody is smoking. I've even smelled cigarettes while I'm in bed. Nobody smokes in our house. It's CRAZY!

There are definitely silver linings since Garrett's passing. I've met people and had experiences and opportunities presented to me that never would have happened had it not been for the steps I've taken in my healing process. Our kids are together. They connect us with other parents. My Garrett and Garrett Savoie pretty much pushed his mom Laurie and I right into each other at a meeting. I had never met her, and I didn't know anything about her child. I overheard her telling another mom that her daughter got a tattoo that day, her 18th birthday, in memory of her brother. Something just then made me look. OMG! The tattoo was "Love, Garrett" in her son's handwriting. I almost fell over. I had to show her my goddaughter's tattoo, in memory of our Garrett. It was "Love, Garrett", only hers was in cursive. From that moment on, Laurie pretty much became my sister from another Mister. We have so many stories that deal with our connections, other groups we're in, experiences, special projects that I create and drag her into (and the rolling of her eyes when I simply say this is what we're doing). There are no coincidences.

I know it doesn't seem possible. Especially to those of you who are so new to this journey that totally sucks donkey balls. BUT... I am happy. Garrett has helped me become a much better version of me. I realize what really matters in life. Things that seemed important before are just NOT. I keep negativity out of my life. I'm not afraid to be honest and tell people how I feel. I love being a Shining Light Parent who can help others. I treasure every moment that I have with my boys, the rest of the family, and my amazing friends who have been there through it all. "Things" just don't matter. Relationships and experiences are what matter.

When I tell people about Helping Parents Heal, this is how I describe it. There are many grief groups. Most of them focus on loss; after all, your loss is the reason you joined a group. Losing a child is very sad. It ABSOLUTELY IS VERY SAD. However, in Helping Parents Heal, we focus on OUR KIDS. We share everything about their lives when they were still here and also about what they've done and things that have happened since they transitioned. We get to know everyone's kids' personalities and hear funny stories. It's so uplifting.

It takes a while to get there. When you come to your first few meetings, your grief is still raw and new, and it's a very sad time. We all remember exactly how you're feeling. When Shining Light Parents share their stories and the validations they've gotten from their kids, it makes you feel lighter. There are smiles and laughter and so much love and support. Everyone feels better after coming to the first meeting. It really is very comforting to be around others who have been there and can honestly say they know how you feel. Nobody else could possibly understand what we've gone through. The local group of HPH has become my Second Family. They helped in opening my mind up to so much more than what we see here on earth. Sometimes it takes a tragedy, or traumatic event, to force you to want to believe that there is more. AND THERE IS!!

-Written by Garrett's Shining Light Mom and HPH Presenter, Michelle Ziff

Devon Harper Hollahan

Devon Hollahan was born early in the morning of May 27, 1987. The first time his grandmother saw him, she said, "He looks at me like he already knows me." Did Devon and his grandma know each other in a previous life? Were we all part of a family unit? We started thinking about these things early in our journey as parents. Little did we know what an amazing journey we were about to experience.

As a young child, Devon was quiet, introspective, and occasionally compulsive in his behavior. He would shoot hundreds of basketball shots from the same spot in our driveway. He would incessantly pace or throw balls or other objects against his bedroom wall. At school, he was sometimes withdrawn and didn't interact much with his classmates. He was, however, a voracious reader, always with a good book at hand. At six, he became interested in dinosaurs, learning everything he could about them. From there his interests moved to sports. Basketball and baseball became his passions! We followed our local Phoenix Suns and Arizona Diamondbacks and attended as many games as we could. Devon became somewhat of a statistics nerd. His mornings usually consisted of him poring over the previous days' box scores as he munched on his Cheerios, committing as much to memory as he could.

When Devon was 12 our family took a vacation to Boston along with Lynn's parents. Devon and I were invited to join his Grandpa Norm and several executives from Norm's company at a Boston Red Sox game held at famous Fenway Park. During the bus ride to and from the ballpark, Devon entertained the other guests with little-known facts and figures about the Red Sox players. While the other invitees were astounded by the depth and breadth of young Devon's detailed knowledge, his proud father sat back and took it all in!

As with many children, Devon's social skills improved as he matured. He acquired some close friends in high school and became more active in his extracurricular pursuits. He developed a true love of all things musical. He grew proficient on the guitar and dabbled in electronics. I would hear strange sounds coming from his bedroom, walk into his room/studio, and see computers hooked up to keyboards by a nest of cables with Devon manipulating the various elements to create the desired effect. One afternoon, I came home from work to be greeted by the notes of "Lady Madonna," by the Beatles. The funny thing was the music sounded "live". The funnier thing was, to the best of my knowledge at the time, I was the only Beatles-loving piano player in the house. Imagine my surprise when I walked into our living room to see Devon sitting at the piano, his laptop propped on top, playing the complex tune! I asked him, "When did you learn how to play the piano, and who in their right mind starts with Lady Madonna?" He casually pointed to his laptop. "There's this cool new thing called YouTube and it has piano lessons on it!"

In college, however, Devon truly came into his own. He did so well in his chosen field of study that one of his professors asked him to become a teaching assistant, giving him the responsibility of conducting classes on an occasional basis. Although the challenge left him unsure at first, Devon took to this new task quickly and was apparently pretty good at it! Aside from his scholastic career, he began to develop a passion for photography. His camera was his constant companion. He joined the University of Arizona Ultimate Frisbee Club and, in addition to playing, became the team's unofficial photographer.

During Devon's college years we, as a family, were fortunate to be able to travel internationally, and Devon's whimsical style often surfaced in his photos. The highlight of his collegiate experience was an internship in London the summer before his senior year, when he had the opportunity to live, work and bond with 20 of his classmates. I truly believe this experience changed his life. He spoke of his friends often and enthusiastically and had some amazing adventures with them while abroad.

After Devon graduated from the University of Arizona, I went down to Tucson to help him gather his belongings for the move back to Scottsdale. That evening, as we shared a great dinner at a local Mexican restaurant, Devon informed me that while he understood that his degree in Business Economics was a valuable professional asset, his true heart was in teaching. Neither Lynn nor I were surprised since Lynn comes from a long line of educators.

Shortly after Devon's graduation, Lynn and I traveled with friends to the British Virgin Islands for a week-long catamaran trip. Most of that week was spent beyond the range of cell phone signals, so Devon and his sister, Kelsey, were basically left to fend for themselves while we were off playing. Upon our return, we found out that Devon had applied, been accepted, and sent payment from his own bank account to the TEFL (Teaching English as a Foreign Language) School in Prague, Czech Republic. His newest adventure was about to begin!

Overseas in Prague, Devon was once again in his element. The 25 students taking the course formed an instant bond. They studied, dined, partied, and traveled together. One of the course instructors confided to me later that he had never seen another group connect as closely as this class did.

Dear friends of ours traveled to Prague in the fall of 2009 and reported back that they had never seen Devon so relaxed and happy. Shortly after their visit, Devon mentioned to us that he would be traveling to Frankfurt, Germany with an acquaintance to see a performance of the American band, Portugal the Man. It would be a quick weekend trip, with an overnight stay at a hostel in Frankfurt. We usually called Devon on Sunday mornings, but on this particular Sunday, November 22, 2009, he didn't answer his phone. We weren't concerned since he was a seasoned world traveler, and we knew he had been out of town.

Later that day, at around 3 pm, we received the call that would change the course of our lives. Devon's traveling companion called from Prague to tell us that he and Devon had become separated on their way back to the hostel after the concert. He presumed Devon would show up later, and when he didn't, his friend headed back to Prague, thinking Devon had caught an earlier train. Upon arriving in Prague and not finding Devon there either, the friend was concerned that our son was missing and was calling to let us know. Again, we didn't panic at this point because of Devon's extensive travel experience, though it was unlike him to be out of touch with his friends and family for this long.

Later that evening, as Lynn lay in bed, a light crossed the ceiling of our bedroom, and the word *river* unexpectedly entered her mind. The experience was powerful enough that she burst out of our bedroom to share it with me. Her interpretation of the sign was that Devon was in the river. Not having any experience with "signs", I had no idea what to think, but I didn't like the sound of this.

A couple of days later, Lynn called the "spiritual bookstore" to get a referral for a psychic. As luck would have it, there just happened to be a couple on staff. Lynn and our daughter Kelsey sat down with one of these Lightworkers who told them that Devon was "fine", but it would be four weeks before we found him. Despite Lynn's vision of the ball of light and the sound of the word River, she decided that if Devon was indeed "fine", it meant he must be "alive".

Over the next week, Devon's disappearance took on a life of its own. Despite the fact that no evidence had surfaced anywhere regarding the whereabouts of our son, the local and national media got involved. I think the biggest "angle" to our story was that it took place right before the holidays. On Thanksgiving, we had a camera crew from The Today Show in our home. The following day, we did live interviews with all three major television networks. The disappearance of a quiet, somewhat shy, and unassuming young man had become national news and was about to go global.

After this flurry of media appearances, it was clear that there was very little else we could do from home. Devon was missing in Germany, and it was time to go over there to find him. The Sunday after Thanksgiving I boarded a plane to Frankfurt. When I disembarked, I was greeted by a member of the US State Department, who alerted me to the fact that a significant number of journalists were waiting inside the terminal for a statement. As I navigated my way through the phalanx of reporters and did my best to answer the questions being thrust at me, I couldn't help but wonder how my family and I had arrived at this surreal existence. This strange situation became even more so when I went to check into my hotel in downtown Frankfurt. When I presented myself to the front desk staff, the young man at the reception desk excused himself to pull the general manager out of a meeting so he could personally greet me. He introduced himself and said, "Mr. Hollahan, we know why you are here, and we want you to know that the top floor of our hotel has been reserved for you and your party for as long as you need to be here – compliments of the Marriott Corporation." I was flabbergasted and did my best to express my thanks for his compassion and generosity, but I'm sure it was woefully inadequate. It was the first of many amazing acts of kindness we were to experience in Frankfurt.

Once in my room, I unpacked and set up my computer for a video chat session with Lynn and Kelsey. My most memorable part of that chat was Lynn's comment asking me what I was doing to my forehead. Apparently, I was unconsciously making some type of motion that was out of character enough to catch Lynn's attention Amazingly enough, a few hours later, a local healer and medium, Debra Martin, called Lynn, introduced herself and said, "I need to tell you that your husband's deceased father is coming to him through his forehead."

For the next several weeks, Debra became Lynn's personal spiritual advisor, bringing through several signs and synchronicities that Lynn latched onto – hard! For Lynn, Debra became a safe space, someone she could share her deepest feelings and fears with because, at that time, there were no emotional attachments between the two of them. And then one day Debra uttered the words that became our family motto: "The raven will show you the answer." I don't think Debra even knew exactly what that statement meant, and I know for sure that we didn't either! Interestingly, we were contacted by numerous mediums from around the world and almost everyone referenced a raven or blackbird as being an important messenger for us.

A couple of days later, Lynn and Kelsey joined me in Frankfurt, and over the course of the next three weeks we did everything we could to find Devon. We had volunteers from the community place flyers at train stations and in public gathering places. We formed search parties and inspected various neighborhoods at all hours of the day and night. We had meetings with the police to discuss their findings.

As time went by, evidence grew that Devon might indeed be in the river. As sad as it was, we booked a flight to Prague to go meet Devon's classmates and collect some of his belongings from his apartment. His friends shared stories about Devon's time in Prague, accompanied by laughter and many tears. Leaving Prague, we knew in our hearts that we could do no more in Europe, and it was time to go home.

On our last day in Frankfurt, Lynn felt a strong need to bid goodbye to our son. On a cold, gray, winter's day in Germany, Lynn, Kelsey, and I walked down to the Main River. Once there, Kelsey stayed up near street level while Lynn and I descended to the park area that lined both sides of the river. Though we were walking side by side, our thoughts separated us as we tried to absorb the events of the last month: the heartbreak, anguish, anger, and confusion. We also reflected on the outpouring of love from friends, family, and total strangers from around the globe who got caught up in our story; on the compassion of the staff at the Marriott Hotel, and on the sacrifices of the employees of my firm in Europe, who gave up their precious weekends to offer food and lodging and help in the search for our son.

While we wandered around the park, trying to deal with the emotions of our new reality, a large black raven flew down and landed on the grass between us. The raven locked eyes with Lynn and then looked to the river, not once, but several times. Was this the bird the mediums had told us about? Lynn believed it was, and even skeptical me was having a hard time discounting the significance of this creature. As if to add an exclamation point to the experience, as Lynn walked down a short flight of stairs to a platform where she could place her hand in the water, the raven accompanied her, taking a drink each time. She knew then without a doubt that this was "her" bird and was indeed giving her the answer. Unfortunately, it was not the answer for which we had hoped.

As the three of us walked back to the hotel, arm-in-arm, silent, grieving, our cheeks wet with tears, not knowing what the future now held, we noticed hundreds of blackbirds lining the building rooftops above us on either side of the street. As we approached, the birds flew down, gathered around us and then flew as one toward the river.

The day we arrived home, we heard from the US State Department that Devon's body had been recovered from the Rhine River, 60 kilometers downstream from Frankfurt. They had found him the very day that the raven showed us the answer --December 22 -- 4 weeks to the day after Lynn's first reading with the psychic, just as she had predicted.

On Christmas day, we reluctantly accepted an invitation to join extended family members for an early holiday dinner. It was easily the most awkward gathering of our lives. Devon's name did not come up, the 800-pound gorilla in the room was ignored, and we put our heads down and tried to finish up and leave as quickly as humanly possible. As we finished our meal, Lynn asked me to read aloud an email I had recently received from Trish, one of Devon's TEFL instructors in Prague. In the letter, she described Devon's qualities as a student and a person. She talked about the special bonds between his classmates throughout the course. Lastly, she mentioned that ever since she was little, whenever a close relative passed, she would receive a "vision" of that relative and that these visions brought her peace and comfort.

She went on to describe her recent vision of Devon, which took place in downtown Prague during the Christmas market. She mentioned the smell of the pine trees and holiday food from the stalls and how the snow was lightly falling. Across the square, in a crowd of people, she picked out Devon, and he walked towards her. She described the clothing he was wearing, his backpack and other traveling essentials, and as he drew close, she asked him, "Devon, where have you been? Don't you know everyone is looking for you?" He replied, "Tell them that I am fine and that I've been with them the whole time!"

As you might expect, I was unable to read the email straight through, owing to the knot in my throat and the tears flowing continuously down my cheeks. But when I was able to compose myself, I looked across the dining table to find Lynn's mother staring incredulously at me. She glanced at her husband (Lynn's stepdad) and asked if he would be willing to read a letter he had just received from his granddaughter, Sarah.

In the letter, Sarah described her own recent vision. She was in a Christmas market in a medieval city. She mentioned the cobblestone streets, the smell of food and pine trees and a crowd of people from which Devon emerged. As Devon drew near, she described the clothes he was wearing--the exact outfit he was wearing in Trish's vision. Sarah also asked Devon the same question as Trish had and received the same answer; "Tell them I am fine, and I've been with them the whole time." Trish and Sarah didn't know each other and when the dates of the letters were compared, the visions were found to have occurred on the same evening, 11 time zones away from each other and, "coincidentally", while Lynn, Kelsey and I were walking through the Prague Christmas markets. Devon really HAD been with us the whole time! This was the first synchronicity that I had experienced, but the proximity to Devon's passing reduced the impact it might otherwise have had. There was more to come.

The first several weeks of our new journey found Lynn, Kelsey, and I occupying the same home, but infrequently interacting. For my part, I was simply unable to deal with the constant pain I saw in the eyes of my wife and daughter. We were lost as a family and none of us knew how to cope. The endless days found us in different rooms of the house, the doors closed to isolate us from each other. On one particular day, Lynn was at her computer, I was in our music room, and Kelsey was holed up in Devon's bedroom. While working on her computer, Lynn received an email from Debra Martin saying that Devon was messing around with Kelsey's computer, causing words to repeat and switch to all caps. Lynn thought this was interesting and forwarded the email to Kelsey. Within seconds, Kelsey came bounding out of Devon's room confirming the odd behavior of her computer! She had even rebooted her laptop a few moments earlier in an effort to correct the problem!

Debra continued to reach out to us via emails, phone calls, and personal visits with messages and signs from Devon. Devon, it seemed, was taking over Debra's life with constant messages for his family. We also became more in tune with the signs we were receiving, such as lights going on and off, the stereo turning on when we would talk about Devon, items mysteriously jumping off shelves, random phone calls from Devon's phone with "no one" on the other line, orbs in photos, etc. Even our dog seemed to be aware of Devon's presence. And oh, there were LOTS of Ravens showing up in our lives.

Debra filled another important role for us: she introduced us to Mark and Susie Ireland. Mark is one of the founders of HPH. Shortly after meeting the Irelands, we were introduced to Elizabeth Boisson and the rest of the early members of this esteemed group. This was a true blessing for Lynn and me. We had been to a couple of grief group meetings and had come away from each not only NOT feeling better, but more lost and confused than before! With Helping Parents Heal, we had finally found "our people"! In the early days of HPH, we tried to schedule social gatherings as frequently as possible. These events usually took place at local restaurants and were always boisterous and joyful! The night of our first get-together, I commented to no one in particular that I would be amazed if anyone else in the establishment could guess what bond the seven couples at our table shared. Couples whose children have passed are not supposed to be having fun, laughing, telling stories, sharing memories, and joking with one another, right? Well, this group was celebrating their children and the higher vibrations were palpable! They continue to this day.

For Lynn and me, this coming November will mark the twelfth anniversary of Devon's transition. For the 28 years we spent together prior to his passing, we thought we had the perfect life. We loved our family and each other, we traveled the world, we laughed, and we shared everything! After everything we have experienced since, we have a different definition of perfect, and we wouldn't trade places with anyone. Our love for one another grows by the day. Many of our friends and family members have willingly joined us on this amazing journey and our bonds with each of them are truly remarkable. We enjoy the richest of lives and engage fully with every opportunity we are given. As Baba Ram Dass said, "We're all just walking each other home." Blessings....

-Written by Devon's Shining Light Dad, Helping Parents Heal Board Member, Presenter and HPH Caring Listener, Jeff Hollahan, and Devon's Shining Light Mom and Head of Caring Listeners, Lynn Hollahan

Brandon Blake Donald Ireland

Our youngest son, Brandon Ireland, was born on September 30, 1985, and passed on January 10, 2004. Brandon always put the needs and concerns of others before his own—he was naturally empathetic, compassionate, kind, and considerate. A good-natured young man, Brandon was tall, with long curly brown hair and eyes that reflected his loving and caring nature. He brought a special joy to our home with his lighthearted humor and positive outlook. Brandon always kept things in their proper perspective and reminded us all of what was truly important. He never got too excited or upset over the countless issues of daily life.

Brandon showed a strong aptitude for mathematics, which correlated to his exceptional musical skills. His mathematical ability also led him to an interest in physics, which he intended to study in college. Brandon's first love was the bass guitar. He was an accomplished musician, having studied the instrument since the age of twelve and began playing in a band with his instructor, Todd Hogan, several years later. Brandon also loved to play paintball with his buddies and to hike in the mountains behind our home in the Arizona desert. So, it is fitting that his transition happened while doing what he loved—hiking with his friends.

January 10, 2004, started like any other Saturday. I sipped coffee and scanned the newspaper while my wife Susie took her walk and Brandon sat glued to the computer. My older son Steven, who had moved out a few months earlier, was in his apartment getting ready for work. Like most eighteen-year-old kids, Brandon spent endless hours on the computer, surfing the Web and playing games. Later that morning he moved on to his first love, the bass guitar. Beckoned by the sounds of his instrument I strolled into our living room, picked up my Fender Stratocaster, and began to accompany him.

At approximately 10:30 that morning, I grew particularly uneasy about my son's plans for the day. He and his friends intended to embark on a very difficult hike to the summit of the McDowell

Mountains. At the time, I sensed that something was going to go very wrong during the hike, feeling that circumstances could possibly even conspire to end Brandon's life. Since my normal tendency was to worry, I dismissed my feelings as those of an anxious parent.

But due to my overwhelming sense of apprehension, I could not resist asking Brandon to stay home, noting somewhat lamely that it was far too windy for such an expedition. In response, he looked at me and said firmly, "We're going, Dad," as if to convey the message "Stop worrying."

By now I have come to realize that on occasions when my intuition is activated, focused upon a specific issue, I feel a sense of certainty or knowledge that does not arise from any external source. This sense is similar to a memory, although my awareness involves events that have not yet occurred or have taken place without my previous knowledge. In the case of Brandon's hike, the feeling was extraordinarily strong. I was overcome with what I could only describe as a wave of energy. It felt as if another presence were around me. Along with this came a sense of extreme urgency surrounding an impending risk to Brandon. Again, I dismissed this as imagined worry.

So, despite my premonitions and warnings, Brandon and his friends began their trek toward the McDowell Mountains. On that particular day, ominously strong winds drove pollutants from the Greater Phoenix Valley toward the mountains. The impure air made the vigorous climb all the more stressful, and Brandon began feeling poorly. Stuart Garney, his best friend, told me that Brandon rested to try and regain his strength. He also used his prescription inhaler in a desperate attempt to alleviate his deteriorating condition, even though asthma did not seem to be the culprit. Frankly, the boys didn't know what was wrong, because Brandon's symptoms were so unusual, including dizziness, numb limbs, and an irregular heartbeat. Unfortunately, the rest break and inhaler proved ineffective, and Brandon's condition grew progressively worse.

Later in the day, my cell phone rang, and I was momentarily relieved, thinking it might be Brandon. When I looked at the display on my phone, I saw that the call was coming from my older son Steven. My worst fears were about to be confirmed.

Steven was relaying a message from Brandon's buddies, who had called him on their cell phone from the mountainside. The boys had been unsuccessful in attempts to reach us at home and didn't know my cell number. Ironically, because of my earlier premonition, I'd placed a piece of paper with my number on it in Brandon's backpack. I vividly remember Brandon saying, "Dad, you don't need to give me this, I know your cell phone number." I responded, "Yes, but the other boys don't." As it turns out, while Stuart and another boy, Chris, had been with Brandon since he first started feeling ill, the boys who had cell phones were farther up the mountain and so had no access to my number. Seeing Stuart waving for help in the distance, they called my other son Steven.

My wife and I were across town at the time, so we jumped into my car and drove home. All the way, I feared that we might lose Brandon, but I tried to hold out hope. As we came within two miles of home, my heart sank as fire trucks, ambulances, helicopters, and a horde of spectators came into view. The first police officer we encountered introduced us to the Chaplain, which made my hopes fade even further. I felt light-headed with fear. Approximately thirty minutes after our arrival we were informed that our son had passed. Shortly thereafter, we viewed Brandon's lifeless body in the back of an ambulance and prayed with the Chaplain, all the while weeping uncontrollably.

In the days after Brandon passed, Susie, Steven, and I remained in a state of shock. We each fluctuated between periods of isolation and interaction, but nothing we did brought much relief or rest.

The response I found most helpful and gave me hope during this time was reflecting on the extraordinary things I'd experienced in life. You see, I come from a family in which spiritual gifts such as psychic phenomena are prevalent. My family tree includes many individuals who have possessed various forms of extrasensory perception, or ESP. These capabilities first appeared in my great-grandmother, Mary Burch-Fling, who had "hunches" and "feelings in her bones" that were usually on target. My grandmother Margaret Fling, my father Richard Ireland, and my uncle Robert Ireland were also similarly gifted, as well as other family members. In addition to psychic abilities, my father, uncle, and grandmother were endowed with the gift of Mediumship, also known as "Spirit Communication".

Just two days after Brandon's passing, I received the first message about my son's well-being in the next realm. At about 2 PM on Monday, January 12, 2004, I was standing in the Desert Hills mortuary when my cell phone rang. Seeing that the call was from my uncle, I immediately felt both hope and anxiety. Knowing that my uncle was a gifted Psychic-Medium, like my deceased father, Richard Ireland, I listened with great anticipation.

My uncle proceeded to tell me, "I tried to make a connection last night but got nothing. This morning, however, your dad came to me during meditation. He told me that Brandon's heart failed due to a lack of oxygen, and while he experienced shortness of breath, Brandon suffered no pain. When Brandon first left his body, he was confused, but your dad came to meet him and helped him adjust. Brandon also had a message for you and Susie. He wants you to know that you were the best parents he ever could have had."

At the time I spoke to my uncle, little was known of the cause of Brandon's death. The authorities would not share any information with us, or were even willing to speculate about what had happened. A week later I spoke to the physician who performed the autopsy. She confirmed that Brandon's death was attributed to a severe asthma attack that led to a decrease in his blood oxygen level and ultimately resulted in cardiac arrest, matching my uncle's explanation. To try and process more oxygen, Brandon's lungs had ballooned to the point of nearly touching at his sternum. This condition, she told us, occurs only in cases of drowning and severe asthma.

I later asked my uncle if he could elaborate on the form his communication with my father took. In response, he shared the following: "When your dad came to me after Brandon's passing, I was doing my morning meditation, which is how I start every day. As you know, I see and hear Spirit very clearly. When I talk to anyone in spirit, it is just a normal two-way conversation—the same as you and I talking. Your dad looks just like himself and sounds exactly as he always has. I have talked with him many times since he passed on."

So here I was, drawn back into the world of my father and his family—a world of spirit communication, signs, and synchronicity. But I was happy to be there, and it felt like home. I was not left to suffer or rely solely on blind faith; I was given instead the certainty of personal experience. My journey was just beginning.

My father, Richard Ireland, was a magnetic and spiritual man who won people's hearts with his open and caring nature while capturing their minds with his profound psychic gifts. In 1960, he founded the *University of Life Church* which he referred to as "Inter-denominational". Born with rare abilities mirroring "The Gifts of the Spirit" the Apostle Paul speaks of in the New Testament, my father's ministry naturally leaned on scripture, but parishioners found the demonstrations of remarkable phenomena most meaningful and validating.

My father's abilities included clairvoyance, precognition, and spirit communication. His trademark demonstration was "blindfold billet", where he would cover his eyes with ten strips of medical tape sealed tightly around his eye sockets and nose, topped with three opaque black blindfolds—and more tape on top of that. Ironically, my father's eyesight was so poor he couldn't pass a driver's license eye exam.

Once my father was blindfolded, questions written on small pieces of paper called "billets" were delivered to the pulpit. My father would rummage through the papers, touching individual billets, *feeling* where to go first. After this, he would call out the first and last name of the person who wrote the message. After identifying the recipient, he went on to share a wide range of personal information—touching on things like jobs, relationships, and pending births. These validations were delivered with a high degree of accuracy and specificity, and my father frequently referenced things not written on the paper.

Sometimes people would receive messages from deceased loved ones, messages that resonated with recipients because of the precise nature of the information shared. And since my father delivered compelling information to at least half of those in attendance, any suggestion of audience plants was quashed. People believed, but more importantly, *I believed.* Or, I should say, *I knew.*

I experienced these phenomena as part of my daily life—not only as a detached observer, where I watched my father deliver accurate information against all odds to strangers, but also in our home where he used his preternatural insights for familial purposes. My teenaged older brother did not appreciate my father intuiting and halting his beer acquisition methods. Nor was my mother pleased when Dad busted her for consuming a hamburger secretly at a time when she'd committed to being a vegetarian.

Other people who had received messages from my dad shared their confirmations with me firsthand. These messages involved not only information gleaned from clairvoyance, but also specific predictions about future events that subsequently came to pass.

My father had a deep love for humanity, and his sense of compassion extended far beyond the church. He demonstrated his abilities in venues ranging from conference rooms to nightclubs and Las Vegas showrooms, a plurality that left some parishioners uneasy. But my father felt it was important to reach *all* people with the message, "You are more than a body", as he felt this theme was the cornerstone of spirituality. By reaching out to the secular world, he was able to counsel celebrities such as Mae West, Darrell Zanuck, Glenn Ford, Amanda Blake, and even the Eisenhowers.

Providing an example of how my father used his abilities to help people, Berdenia Faye Broes shared the following story with me: He saved my daughter's life in 1976 when she was twelve years old. She had been so sick—her throat literally closed up and it looked like green mold. She was at the UCLA Medical Center in Irvine, and I was so concerned. There were specialists involved, she'd undergone a battery of tests, and they'd flown in doctors from Boston and Houston and no matter what they did or how many tests they ran they could not figure out what was wrong with her.

As a last resort, I called Richard. He said, "She has a staph infection and it's throughout her system." He then provided a set of instructions for the doctors to follow in treating her. I wrote everything down and took it to the doctor. When I shared it, the doctor asked me, "Where did you get this information?" I responded, "If I told you, you'd think I am crazy, but please just check this out." The doctors followed Richard's instructions and it turned out that he was exactly right. My daughter had been in the hospital for 2 ½ months, but she came out of it.

I loved my father but deliberately chose a different, more stable path than a life centered on the metaphysical. Plus, I didn't feel that I possessed the same abilities, nor did I share his passion. But under my current circumstance—Brandon's passing, and my father's legacy to consider--I embarked on a spiritual journey that unfolded in a way I could never have imagined. Not only did it lead to my publishing three books, chronicling experiences supporting the Afterlife, but also to co-founding Helping Parents Heal in partnership with Elizabeth Boisson.

Reflecting on the past, I'd never considered the possibility that Brandon might transition early in life. My wife Susie, however, recalled an instance that made her think Brandon had some inner suspicion about what was to come. At around the age of sixteen, he was fitted for braces. Before the procedure, he told Susie, "Mom, I don't need these". It never occurred to her at the time, but after his passing Susie recalled the conversation and sensed that Brandon may have had an intuitive feeling that he wouldn't be around long enough to benefit from braces. A possible confirmation of this came to me during a reading with Allison Dubois, when she stated, "Your son is saying that you couldn't have saved him. He says that he never felt he would grow old—he had the sense that his life would be short."

I also recall a couple of interesting exchanges between Brandon and my father, where I felt like my dad knew something about Brandon that he wasn't telling me. It wasn't what he said, but how he said it and how he looked at Brandon. If he was aware that Brandon would pass at a young age, I can understand why he wouldn't have shared that information with me, especially if it was a matter of destiny that couldn't be altered.

With Brandon's passing, I was inspired to probe deeper, investigating questions about life, death, and life after death. Drawing on my past, I realized that my father had wielded a significant influence on my life and my overall perspective. As mentioned earlier, I was comforted by memories of the remarkable events I'd experienced growing up. This led me to embark on a journey with both spiritual and empirical implications. It involved a lot of reading and research, but also reaching out to other sources that I could examine objectively. In the course of my study, I observed top mediums like Allison Dubois, Laurie Campbell, and others under controlled conditions and found them capable of sharing specific, meaningful information about Brandon and other deceased loved ones. These sessions were conducted in a manner that afforded the mediums little or nothing in the way of sensory cues or information in advance.

As an example, Allison Dubois knew nothing about my son Brandon's passing, but her first words to me were: "I see a son connected to you. I'm not sure if he passed or if I'm seeing a son who is yet to be born." She then asked, "Did he have breathing problems? He's highlighting his lungs—as if breathing was heavy or difficult when he passed." She then asked me if my son had asthma or any problems with his lungs.

On the heels of that, Allison added, "Your son who passed had fluid in his lungs, or at least that is what it feels like. It's as if it was so hard to breathe his lungs might as well have been filled with water." This was exactly what the physician who performed the autopsy had reported to me when she stated that Brandon's condition only occurred in cases of severe asthma attacks and drownings. Allison softened her message by sharing, "He says, 'No more, it's not like that now'." Allison also referenced my father being with my son:

"Your dad mentions 'having the boy.' Your son is with your dad, and he says, 'That's how it should be'."

Continuing with my father, providing a mind-bending validation, Allison said, "I see him signing a book and handing it over to you. I believe this was his book and he is handing it over to you—do you understand this?" Just a week earlier I had been contacted by one of my dad's former acquaintances, who handed me an unpublished manuscript authored by my father in 1973.

Before this call, I was completely unaware that the work *Your Psychic Potential: A Guide to Psychic Development* even existed. Just before his death, my father asked this friend to hold the manuscript for safekeeping, which made perfect sense since I was then living in another state. No one was aware that I'd received the work—Allison certainly had no way of knowing about it. Subsequently, in 2011, I was able to get my father's book published.

My family members and I have experienced an interesting series of phenomena that indicate contact with or communication from my son Brandon, as well as from other loved ones. I can only share a few examples here, but those interested in knowing more can check out my books, *Soul Shift: Finding Where the Dead Go* and *Messages from the Afterlife*.

One of the most profound instances occurred six months after Brandon's passing and involved my wife Susie, who felt our son's presence and saw him as a shadow figure to her right, through her peripheral vision. The very next day a musician friend, James Linton, called to report a virtually identical occurrence, where he felt a presence and saw a shadow figure.

When he called to tell her about his experience, James was unaware of Susie's encounter the prior day. He intuitively felt the figure was Brandon and acknowledged him verbally at the time. After doing so,

James was inspired to compose and record a song that he felt was directly influenced by our son, through a deeply emotional process of channeling. Ironically, James had borrowed Brandon's bass guitar and played it on the recording. Referencing the completed song, entitled, "The Other Side," James said, "It's the best song I've ever written, but I didn't write it."

On January 28, 2014, Susie and I received a stellar reading from Mollie Morningstar. She addressed many issues specific to my mother and other loved ones who had passed, but the most touching and compelling validation involved a message from Brandon. Through Mollie, Brandon passed along the following information about his brother Steven's upcoming wedding, which was to take place on May 9, 2014. She noted that Brandon was the "real best man", but it was okay for someone else to stand in. Mollie then referenced several specific future events.

Mollie said, "Brandon is showing me that Steven will be wearing a really nice suit at the wedding. It's not quite a tuxedo, but it's close." She added, "Brandon now pulls something out of a pocket in the suit. I believe Steven is planning on having something that belongs to Brandon in his pocket and on his person at the wedding. It's like a little picture or something—but there is something physical and tangible that you can touch that Steven has on his person. It's some kind of memento. Brandon also makes the point that he is going to be there, and he is saying 'Two o'clock'."

Five months later, on his wedding day, Steven wore a very nice suit—not a tuxedo. That afternoon one of the groomsmen, David Butcher, handed me a small box and said it was a gift from Liz Rohe, a friend who couldn't make the trip. Inside the box, I found six small pins that could be slid into a suit-coat pocket, each with a framed portrait of Brandon. And at approximately 2:00 PM (14:00 hours) my wife Susie first saw the pins, which Steven, the groomsmen, and I wore in our suit breast coat pockets. There is no way to fake a prediction—it either comes to pass, or it doesn't. Brandon was there with us.

There is more to the universe than our five physical senses tell us, and the religion of materialism/physicalism is a lie. Mind precedes matter. The "double-slit" physics experiment revealed the "observer effect", which demonstrates that the mind affects matter. And "entanglement", another experimentally proven phenomenon, implies that we are part of an interconnected universe. The truth is that matter is nothing but energy in vibration. This was suggested by ancient sages and has since been confirmed by modern quantum physicists.

While I believed in the hereafter from the beginning, my new experiences have provided me with a sense of expanded awareness. They have also yielded new perspectives on the nature of reality that have strongly affected my worldview. So, it goes with the evolution of thinking—a process that is an inherent part of life's experience. I invite you to consider that your mind may be more than your brain, and that your soul just might be more than your body. Brandon has shown us that this is the true nature of things.

-Written by Brandon's Shining Light Dad, Co-Founder of Helping Parents Heal, Chairman of the Board and Presenter, Mark Ireland

Andy "Sunshine" Hull

I am no different from any other parent who cannot wait to talk about their amazing kids; the only difference is that one of my kids, Andy, is in Heaven. As soon as I share the details of my son's present location, people usually stop and take a breath, but nothing will stop me from wanting to talk about my precious child.

No matter how our children pass, we all struggle in the early days anticipating and handling the dreaded conversations. So many questions to maneuver through in these uncharted waters. How many children do you have? How old are they? What do they do now? If you are brave enough to blurt out the reality that you are living with, more questions and comments follow. *How did your child pass? He or she is in a better place. God has a plan. At least you have other children.* It's like a minefield full of emotional explosives! But eventually, with practice, it will become second nature for you to talk about *all* your children, whether they are physically on the planet or "living" in spirit.

And yes, I do believe that with practice, patience, and persistence you can find a place of peace after your child moves on.

So, let me tell you about Andy, my fourth, wonderful son, born to seasoned parents, eleven years after his three siblings, Mike, Beth, and Josh. Even though we weren't planning on more children, Andy felt like a gift and a blessing. Truly, his nickname of Sunshine fit him to a tee, he seemed to brighten any day and make everyone feel better. I would describe Andy as having *joie de vivre*, embracing all that life had to offer him.

His gift of funny impersonations of Smeagol from Lord of the Rings and the crazy lemur in Madagascar who sings, "I like to move it move it" regularly provided us with comic relief. He and his friends created hysterical videos, making funny faces and dancing around. I absolutely love to watch those videos now, reminding me of the joy that he brought to our lives.

Keeping up with his boundless energy was challenging but overall, extremely rewarding and fun. Andy wasn't a kid to sit still or waste hours playing video games. He was always on the move, playing with his friends, riding his bike, or playing sports. The question for us was, how do we keep up with him?

Early on it became apparent that Andy was a gifted athlete. It didn't matter whether he was playing baseball, doing backflips on the wakeboard, or jumping off cliffs at the local swimming hole, he enjoyed it all. Having only twenty-four hours in a day soon became Andy's biggest challenge as there just didn't seem like enough time in a day to squeeze in everything that he wanted to do.

In addition to sports, Andy and his dad, Clay, enjoyed an adventurous journey in scouts together. The very first day, when they met the scout leader who talked nonstop about blasting off rockets, jumping off cliffs into amazing waterholes, shooting off firecrackers and lots of wilderness camping, they knew that they had found a perfect fit. For the next several years, until Andy was almost an Eagle Scout, the two of them enjoyed much time together in the great outdoors.

Most important in Andy's life as well as ours was a deep faith and spiritual walk. As a toddler, Andy often talked about his father. While this sounds normal enough, he would chat away while sitting next to his dad as if he were talking about someone else. We all believed that he was referring to his Heavenly Father which we thought was unusual in someone so young. But whomever he was talking about, Andy was in touch with a spirit world that the rest of us would come to understand better after he left the physical world.

Youth group at church became a place where Andy could grow spiritually and build great relationships with other like-minded kids. In addition, he had great fun at summer and winter church camps, deepening his spirit-filled life, which spilled over to anyone who knew him.

By the time Andy reached high school, he had become quite an accomplished left-handed pitcher. Playing on Varsity baseball as a freshman as well as other club teams, he was a busy boy. Practice and games every day including weekends left little time for anything else. Pitching and hitting coaches were squeezed into tiny spaces of time wherever we could find them.

Not surprisingly, his life totally revolved around baseball, which caused conflicts with his other interests. Anyone who aspires to be a professional athlete will ultimately have to make sacrifices, which can be challenging especially for a young person. But baseball seemed to be what Andy wanted more than anything else, so we did our best to help him achieve his dreams.

He came close to achieving his goal. And yet in the end, multiple factors conspired to lead Andy to complete suicide in the middle of his junior year, 14 days before Christmas, and just two weeks after scouts from all over the country had come to Phoenix, Arizona, to watch him pitch his nasty slider. He was at the top of the world, or so it seemed.

I could list all the factors which contributed to that moment of pain, but I genuinely believe, with all my heart and soul, that none of that matters now. Making decisions to move forward while allowing yourself the time to grieve great loss is critical. It's a tricky juggling act, but our focus must be on our survival and mental health.

The only time that I talk about the triggers which contributed to that fateful day is when I speak to others about the warning signs of suicide. Nothing will change that day, so I try to use what I've learned to help others cope with the challenges that life brings their way in the wake of such an occasion. Accepting the fact that none of us escape from some form of pain and sorrow will help you to better prepare for the inevitable. Preparing in advance, gathering a toolbox full of healthy coping skills, will help you immensely when the tough times do arrive.

Several things helped me on my journey forward after Andy moved on. One of the most uncharacteristic decisions that I made in the first month after Andy passed was to schedule a reading with a local Medium. Such an action was totally out of my comfort zone and absolutely against my religious beliefs. But great pain and trauma can lead us beyond our familiar coping strategies in the hope of finding relief from gut-wrenching anguish.

Susanne Wilson, The Carefree Medium, had been recommended to me by several of my Facebook friends. So, in total secrecy I scheduled an appointment for a reading. I was terrified but couldn't wait to "talk" to my kid. And "talk" we did! At the end of the reading, Andy "said", "My mom is tough as nails, and she will be fine!" And he was right. Here I am.

Before I walked out the door, Susanne said to me, "You should look up a group called Helping Parents Heal and reach out to Elizabeth Boisson. Andy says the group will help you move forward." I left that day still broken in a million pieces but with a glimmer of hope and a tiny spring in my step. I was on my way down a road that none of us would ever want to travel but one that has totally transformed my understanding of what walking in faith and spirit really means. Of course, I am still a work in progress, but leaps and bounds ahead of where I was.

I gave myself permission to see Susanne every six months for two years so that I could have my "intergalactic conversations" with my kid. It was the best therapy that I ever indulged in. In between those readings, I also began my journey with Helping Parents Heal, where I not only began to heal but also forged deep friendships with other

Moms and Dads I met at the meetings. It was essential for me to have others with whom I felt free to talk about Andy and to share my journey with. Friends from my old life tried their best to support me but couldn't possibly understand what I was going through. Some, whom I greatly appreciate, continue to be my friends while others simply moved on. No doubt this new journey of mine was more than they could handle. It isn't for the faint of heart.

During HPH meetings over the next several years, Mediums often volunteered their time to give all of us a chance to "talk" with our kids. Andy showed up many times during those meetings to deliver messages that boosted my spirit and continue to propel me forward.

Besides the various readings at our meetings, we also learned many different methods of calming and expanding our souls through meditation, yoga, reiki, etc. A variety of teachers and authors donated their time to help us take charge of our lives and heal our hearts. Speaking of authors, I can't stress enough the importance of reading as many books as you can. Personally, I read eighty books that first year after Andy moved on. Not only will it enrich your mind, it will also empower you to embrace this precious gift called life. Wouldn't we want this for our kids, to grab all that life has to offer? Without a doubt, I know that Andy wants that for me.

As time clicked by, I felt compelled to write my own story about my journey and all the tools that I used to move forward. I began this project around the summer of the three-year mark after Andy moved and completed it during the summer of year six. Isn't it funny how our measurement of time now seems to be based on the day that our child passed? Everything is now expressed as either before or after.

Writing in general was very cathartic for me, but I felt it especially important to share helpful tips with other parents that would help them heal after such a traumatic experience. My book is called "How to Live When You Want to Die". Catchy title, right? Well, honestly, this was truly the way that I felt early on in my grief process. That being said, mine is an uplifting book that will make you laugh and cry but most importantly will help you on your journey to a better place, a place where you can hopefully honor your child with a life well lived.

It is so important for us to know that our children are okay and happy in their new spiritual form. While we miss their physical presence terribly, we can still have a "relationship" with them. They are still our kids. You just have to be willing to listen, learn, and love them in spirit. If you open your mind and heart, you will hear and see them. It may not be in the way or as much as you want, but the experience of connection can still fill your heart and soul with love.

Do I wish that I could get those precious signs and validations every day? Yes, of course, but that isn't my reality. Some parents receive more than others but isn't that the way life is anyway? Comparing our life with the lives of others can hamper our ability to recover our own happiness and joy. We aren't all living the same existence or having the same experience, so embrace what you have and give thanks. I have found it so helpful to begin every day with gratitude, which gives me a much greater chance for peace and possibly receiving that precious sign from Andy. The more that I practice these mental health skills, the easier life gets.

Like any other Mom or Dad, I would love to turn back the hands of time and have my child back, but that just isn't possible. With the help of the various resources that I have spoken about, I have been able to move forward and ultimately have a greater connection with God and my spiritual guides. I have more work to do here and more love to give. I pray every day that I make Andy proud and live my life being the "Sunshine" for the world.

-Written by Andy's Shining Light Mom, and HPH Presenter, LeAnn Hull

Kyle Aden Erickson

We are Christians, and I am telling you this because what we learned after losing Kyle was not what we had expected; it was a new level of knowing, of believing, and of hope. Our dreams of our son and the signs we have received, have given us new insight into the workings of the 'other side'.

My Husband Glenn and I both grew up in New Jersey, and both pursued successful law enforcement careers. Our plan was to put in our twenty-five years and retire to Arizona. A plan that we thought was perfect.

Kyle was born February 26, 1987, at 11:57pm. He was due on my birthday, March 1, but true to who this new little person was, he was in a hurry to start his life. He was to demonstrate this trait of always being in a rush, searching for new adventures, throughout the course of his life.

Giving birth to my firstborn was the most amazing thing that had ever happened to me. Our lives changed in the most blessed way. When we were picking out names, the movie *The Terminator* had just come out in theatres, and we both liked the good terminator in the movie, whose name was Kyle. So, we decided on Kyle Aden, Aden being my dad's middle name.

Kyle was so easy, a happy baby. I never knew what our lives had been missing until our firstborn arrived.

In 1988, a wonderful thing happened. We were able to buy back my childhood home. My sweet Dad had built it himself, but my parents had sold it some years ago. It was a dream come true for us to be able to raise our boys in the same loving rooms where I had grown up with my sisters.

Our lives were happy and busy with work and our little one. We were both on call, Glenn with his Major Crimes Detective Unit, and me with my K-9 Bomb Dog, Zeus.

We loved being parents so much that we did not want Kyle to be an only child. Then along came his little brother Ethan, known to us as E-Man. He arrived on March 18, 1992, at 12:21 pm.
So, there we were, the four of us, and life was a dream come true. Kyle loved his little brother; they were always together. Both boys played soccer, wrestled, and we were all active in Greyhound rescue. The boys loved our pool and spent hours swimming in the backyard with their dad. Life was good!

The night of Kyle's eighth grade graduation party, Glenn, Kyle, Mason the Greyhound, Katie the Jack Russell, and Wyatt, the parrot, all left on an adventure, driving across this great country to our new future in the wild, wild west of Arizona. Ethan and I were driven to the airport the next morning by my sisters, who were sad to see us go.

The two of us arrived in Phoenix, excited and a little nervous without Glenn and Kyle. In the meantime, Glenn and Kyle were on their excellent adventure. After three very long days they arrived in Phoenix, and we were all grateful to be back together.

We all made fast friends on our cul-de-sac. We found a wonderful church, and the boys started participating in the Youth Group, and really enjoyed it. We settled in and felt at home.

Kyle would be starting his freshman year in Arizona; Ethan was starting fifth grade. Kyle was into BMX bikes, and later we got both boys dirt bikes. Kyle was in Heaven!

Soon it was official, Kyle had a girlfriend! When I saw her for the first time, I was taken aback by how beautiful she was. Kristin became like a member of the family, and she still is.

Kyle's sixteenth birthday was approaching. My Dad had begun showing signs of Alzheimer's when Kyle was around seven. He became obsessed with Kyle. It was difficult to watch his decline. I prayed that God would take him home to end his, and our, suffering. When Dad passed on Kyle's sixteenth birthday, I took it as an answer to my prayers.

Life in our new home was amazing! We vacationed in California and went to the Queen Mary, to San Diego, and to Disneyland, where the Tower of Terror was the best! Catalina is my magical Island. While there, after two glasses of wine, I made the mistake of telling my sixteen-year-old son that he could get a tattoo. It would be the first of many--Kyle had a love affair with tatts!

Kyle's best friend. Luke, and Luke's brother-in-law, Gary, were like family to him. I think he was at their house more than his own. Kyle loved heavy metal, and Luke and Gary had a band, *Unforeseen*. Wherever they played, Kyle would be there. Later Kyle would become the band's guitar tech. Luke told me Kyle always had his back and that they were brothers.

As Kyle's high school graduation was approaching, he talked about becoming an undertaker, of all things! Then at school he met with an Army recruiter and that was all it took. Kyle was all in, but we were not. I remember Sgt. Jones sitting at our kitchen table. I told him that if anything happened to Kyle, I would come after HIM!

We tried to talk Kyle out of joining, but Kyle was determined to enlist, so we gave him our blessing. In July 2005, we said a tearful goodbye to our boy. He was off to basic training at Ft. Sill in Oklahoma. He called us as often as he could, he was homesick, and we missed him. He made it through basic, helping others who were having a more difficult time; some were even suicidal. We all flew out to see him graduate. We were so proud of him.

He soon became PVT Kyle Erickson and was sent to Sether Airbase in Baghdad, Iraq. His unit was the 169th CTC Transportation. He lived in a tent. When he called us, we would ask what he had been doing, and he would answer, "Nothing". His deployment was, as you can imagine, the longest fifteen months of our lives. We would find out later that his "Nothing" was far from nothing. Among the many medals he received, Kyle was singularly hand-picked to recover the British Army's entire fleet of helicopters that had been overturned in a desert storm, operating a crane to do so. He was given the job even though he was the youngest in his unit. For this he received the Army's Commendation Medal. It was one of thirteen medals that our humble son never told us about. We found out only when his Sgt. spoke at his service.

When Kyle finally came home, we took a much-needed breath! I knew his stay would not last, but he was with us for a couple of months, and then he and his girlfriend moved in with friends. I noticed that Kyle was looking more and more like Glenn; they were two peas in a pod--quiet, calm, kind, and thoughtful. Kyle took a job working for a pool company, and all was right with the world. He signed up for the Reserves and learned he would be going back to Iraq in the fall. But he did NOT want to go back.

Friday, April 9, 2010, Kyle called me to chat. He had gotten off work and was at a friend's house out by the pool, laughing as he watched their dogs jump into the water, chasing a ball. He sounded happy that it was the weekend. We ended our conversation as we always did: he would say, " I love you", and I would reply, " I love you so much!"

On April 10, at 7:30 am, Glenn woke up earlier than usual. I remember asking why he was up so early, but he told me, "No reason." Ethan was still sleeping. My phone rang. It was my neighbor, asking me why two police officers were parked in front of our house? I dropped my phone; I knew instantly why, as we were law enforcement. Glenn and I rushed outside, and the officers told us to go back inside. They handed me Kyle's cell phone and his wallet. Apparently, Kyle was driving alone, not wearing a seatbelt, and lost control. His Explorer rolled several times, and he was ejected. Kyle was airlifted, but never regained consciousness.

I believe he was taken right there at the scene of the accident. Our pastor arrived and told us we needed to get to the hospital before the mortuary took him. We left with Ethan and were taken to the hospital Chapel. After a while the Doctor came in and explained how they tried to save Kyle. Eventually we were taken down to see him. That was the longest walk of our lives.

Kyle's service was four days later. Our family arrived and Kristin flew in from Mississippi where she was stationed in the Air Force. They had stayed in touch through the years. After he had broken up with his girlfriend a couple of weeks earlier, I told him to call her, which he did. I believe there was more to their story.

The church was packed. My friend told me later that she had never been to a service with such a diverse group of people--young and old, many high-ranking militaries--more than his Sgt. had ever seen at a service—neighbors, his heavy metal friends, cowboys, his coworkers, and his boss, who had closed the company early so everyone could attend. Several people I didn't even know were there. We were so inspired. On the hardest day of our lives, it was so comforting to hear how many lives Kyle had affected in such positive ways.

Ethan is quiet, calm, and unassuming. Two weeks after Kyle's accident, Ethan came out of his room visibly shaking and crying. He said "Mom, I have to tell you something. Kyle was with us the day we went to the hospital." He then described how Kyle was riding alongside our car on his 'crotch rocket' motorcycle. He said that when we were waiting in the Chapel, Kyle was standing in the doorway, holding his helmet, with the saddest look on his face Ethan had ever seen as he looked in at us. I had no idea what to say; we had just started on this unknown journey.

I had been looking on the internet for answers to why this tragedy had beset our family. On Jamie Clark's website I read how a local Scottsdale man named Mark Ireland had lost a son and subsequently wrote a book called *Soul Shift, Finding Where the Dead Go*. I went out and bought it, and within a few chapters I felt for the first time that we might survive this "new normal.".

I emailed Mark, and the next day he called me. We had a wonderful conversation, and I was crying good tears. He asked if he could give my cell number to Elizabeth Boisson, who had started a local Parent support group,, and of course I said YES! This was how we found Helping Parents Heal. I can't say enough about Mark and Elizabeth, and everyone we have met on this unchosen path. I truly believe that they saved us through their loving support and by showing us how to pay attention to the signs we received from our Kyle. There have been, and will continue to be, many of these signs!

We have had readings. I can tell you that being raised Methodist, this was not something that was embraced in our church. But I wanted real answers. We have had so many amazing signs and validations! Glenn was a skeptic, but Jamie Clark cracked that shell. I believe that true Mediums are gifted by God to give us evidence of our kids continuing on in spirit.

Describing a silver lining is hard for me, I'll be honest. I will speak for myself. I would give back every moment in time since that day to have Kyle back. I would give back every single person who has come into our lives since that day, just to have Kyle back. However, since that is NOT going to happen, every person that has come into our lives and helped us on this very unwelcome journey, *you* are our silver lining.

-Written by Kyle's Shining Light Parents and HPH Founding Members, Nita and Glenn Erickson

The Children of Our Remaining Board Members

Bailey Caroline Durham

Highly anticipated, but unexpected, our journey began in May of 1993. My daughter, Bailey, entered this life with a perfect birth, the first female born in my family in sixty years. As she grew, however, her cognitive development ultimately remained that of a six-month-old. My precious child would die and return countless times within 24 hours due to an adverse reaction to her vaccinations. She became non ambulatory reliant upon me for all her primary and elevated medical needs. Though she was nonverbal, the glimmer in her eyes spoke volumes, and we had our own language, wrapped in love.

Up until she was 21, nineteen years longer than doctors had predicted she would live, every thread of Bailey's life was infused with a particular purpose. That purpose was to create a helping heart in me, her father. I always knew I was meant to help others, but that goal was jump started during Bailey's life by advocating for her medical needs and those of others throughout Louisiana. My work would continue beyond her journey to the other side of her rainbow, through Helping Parents Heal.

I never had any indication that she knew her time here was limited. Every night started with our anticipation that she might not wake. Every morning that she did was a celebration. It's not a choice way to live your life, but your desires as a parent are not often fulfilled.

Certain special people grace this world through a life directed specifically to helping others. Call it part of Bailey's soul plan . . . or call it an inner knowing. Our lack of intelligible communication created a gap, and I lived in that gap for nearly 21 years, waking every 30 minutes during the last seven years of her life to rotate her in bed or having that "Spidey sense" that something was wrong. I lived with a sense of urgency that I should be aware when something went awry. As an added benefit, this also initiated a sense of empathy in me that allowed me to feel when something was wrong in others. Still, I have to admit that knowing how long it took for me to "get it" is proof of my hard head.

On October 1, 2014, at 10:45 AM, Bailey passed. I was fortunate to be with her, as I was for all her firsts and lasts, from her first and last breath to her first and last feeding, and her first and last diaper. Hers was a peaceful passing as I'd had her in hospice at home for a few weeks. She passed on a Wednesday, but it was the previous Monday when a four-hour seizure started her transition. She didn't struggle, and as I lay in her hospital bed with her, telling her the most challenging thing a parent should have to say--"It's alright, baby girl, you can go on"-- Bailey turned her head to me and exhaled her last breath. Her body released, and she was free in spirit.

I was the first to usher my daughter into her new life. I was here with her as she moved into the fullness of spirit. For that, I am forever grateful, and for being her father and her caregiver. Little would I know that a three-year stint after her passing, I would reencounter her. During this time in the valley, I sent forth the eternal question, "Bailey, if you are still here, do something and let me know." Finally, the answer came by her waking me from the darkness of sleep, in the middle of the night, when she knew I was ready: "Dad, would you stop looking?! I'm right here!" This happened not just once but many times and her voice was as audible as if a close friend were sitting next to me.

When Bailey passed, something inside me clicked . . . or clicked off. I no longer felt any fear of death. I no longer felt anger towards others, due to my nature as an empath having been jump started. Maybe the guy that used to cut me off in traffic was really just late for work? I came to respond to events that would usually annoy me with the thought "What is the Eternal Significance of me being mad?" Having crossed the threshold of the worst that could possibly happen to me, I found on the other side a peace that was unusual and comforting. Granted, crossing that threshold took me a few years, as everyone has their own path of grief to travel. Memorializing Bailey by sharing her story became the healing factor that I would need to survive and thrive in the messiness of the death of my firstborn.

Knowing I had to continue to help others in some way, I decided to start an organization for families who had lost a child. I visited other groups whose focus centered on the sentiment of "bereavement." This approach was not for me. Leaving these groups, I felt remarkably worse than when I had arrived, and I knew without a shadow of a doubt that there had to be something better--that I had to *create* something better. Not long after I had started this process, a friend recommended the organization Helping Parents Heal, whose members supported each other in their personal grief but channeled their energies into a celebration of our children's lives.

After a phone call with Elizabeth Boisson, I was sold. I knew I had found a place that facilitated healing, that was peer-led, that didn't exist to profit from the loss of others but connected with the shared emotions that filled their hearts. Helping Parents Heal allowed me to continue to help others in ways I was unable to on my own, and I will be forever grateful.

-Written by Bailey's Shining Light Dad, Helping Parents Heal Board Member and Presenter Jason Durham

Haley Veronica Ford and Wendy Ford

My first daughter, Gwen Dalynn Sanders Ford (Wendy), was born two months premature in January 1967. Due to her undeveloped lungs, her father and I were not given much hope that she would survive. Not only did she survive, but for 37 years, I had the pleasure of seeing my little girl grow up, become a big sister to Ronni, and later a wife and the mother of two children of her own, Patrick and Haley. Although she could be quite stubborn in many ways, she was also very shy. An avid reader, she loved burying herself into a book whenever possible. Nonetheless, she was willing to join public organizations in her role as a mom: she volunteered as both a Girl Scout and Cub Scout leader, a baseball team mother, and treasurer of Liberty School's PTA.

My first granddaughter, Haley Veronica Ford, was born in January 1994. Being a grandmother was (and continues to be) my greatest honor and source of happiness. I treasured every minute I spent with my sweet granddaughter, who called me "Grandmoney", her humorous version of Grandmommy. At just ten years old, Haley was already an accomplished dancer and her life's goal was to be a "rock star". We have a picture of her standing on a coffee table with a hairbrush as her microphone. In 2004, on her tenth (and last) birthday party, she sprayed her hair blue, putting her a little ahead of today's popular trend for strange hair colors. Haley apparently inherited her Grandmommy's sweet tooth, as many empty candy wrappers were later found in her bedroom and backpack, obviously snuck into her room for a private feast.

In April 2004, my beautiful Wendy and Haley were killed by a drunk driver. Wendy died at the scene, but little Haley tried her best to remain with us. Twenty days after the crash, however, she too left her earthly existence. Haley's organs were donated to several people, most notably her heart to a ten-year-old girl in California who is now a beautiful 28-year-old young woman. The crash occurred on my daughter Ronni's birthday; a date that understandably continues to be very bittersweet for our family.

We were never sure why, but Wendy always made it a point to kiss her children every time they climbed into their van. She would squeeze their hands, a clear nonverbal signal that she loved them. On more than one occasion she claimed that she felt like a "target" when driving. She had never been in a previous crash; this was just a fear she shared with her sister Ronni. It was one that became reality when the drunk driver smashed into their vehicle as Wendy was driving that fateful day.

At age 10, our little Haley had no premonitions of death. Her life was perfect, and I am sure she had no reason to think it would not continue that way. We all anticipated her growing up, experiencing the joys of the usual rites of passage, which were ultimately denied her due to the selfish actions of a drunk driver.

What I have learned over these past 17 plus years as I share stores with fellow Shining Light Parents is that "we are all the same, only different". The "same" since we share the sadness of the loss of a child or children. "Different" because of the different manner in which their particular passing came about.

Due to the actual cause of Wendy's and Haley's deaths (having an extremely drunk driver slam into their family van at 60 mph) our family experienced a different kind of shock and disbelief from the parents of a child who passed by illness or who took their own life. The reaction of parents whose child's death was due to a criminal act by a complete stranger is frequently anger. Such anger, however, does not override their belief that their child continues to live in their hearts and is open to continual communication.

My "girls" (as I commonly refer to them, rather than Wendy and Haley separately, as to me, they are now forever bonded), have been very generous with their communications, most often using pennies. My husband Bill (who passed away suddenly in August 2020) often received pennies from them as well. It was our treat to share which one of us got the pennies at any given time. The girls and now Bill ("Grandpy") continue to share these pennies with both friends and family members. I envision the three of them deciding just where they should place that next penny or other sign.

As many HPH parents have also experienced, these signs often appear in strange and unexpected places. One of our first pennies from Haley was found in a vacant dressing room (my other granddaughter Chloe was there for a recital) nearly hidden in a baseboard. The date of the penny was 1994, the year Haley was born. Another penny, highly unlikely to be found on a street near the Vatican, was a U.S. penny--without a doubt a clear message from the girls letting us know they were with us on our European trip.

Leaving pennies in unusual places is the girls' most frequent way of letting us know their spirit remains with us always. Many of my friends find other items (cloud formations, feathers, butterflies, ladybugs, dragonflies, etc.) that likewise warm their hearts. Obviously, no set pattern or item defines gifts from wonderful children; each has their own way of sending us personal signs of love. I have come to realize that we "know" when the message is from our child and the frequency of such communication is usually their choice as well.

It is always so affirming to read posts from other HPH parents when they share their personal messages. Such messages make my heart smile, knowing full well the happiness they have provided.

During one of her many group readings in Phoenix, Arizona, The Carefree medium, Susanne Wilson, shared with the participants that she saw a lot of hearts in the room. I thought perhaps we were included in that group since Haley's heart had been donated. Susanne then added she saw numerous stars and comets. It took me a while to realize that Haley's name was the same as "Halley's Comet". Haley came through and told me that she was okay and that she knew her little brother Patrick was doing well (Patrick and Haley's Daddy survived the crash). It was so wonderful that she was able to assure me that she was fine and knew how we were doing as well.

On July 29, 2020, during one of our HPH Zoom calls, I was fortunate to have a reading from the medium Mark Anthony. He asked if the number 16 or 1 and 6 meant anything to me. At the time, being of course nervous, those two numbers did not ring a bell. Elizabeth later pointed out that at the time of the reading the girls had transitioned 16 years ago. And the 1 / 6 was Haley's birthday, January 6th. The girls sent many other "spot on" messages that evening.... I just needed to focus my attention.

From my personal experience, I cannot identify any specific Silver Lining following Wendy's and Haley's unexpected and untimely deaths, because there are so many. I have had the pleasure of meeting so many wonderful people at HPH and have found them to be as loving as my own family. I know that should I ever need that special hug, whether in person or virtually, it will be provided without delay. Similarly, as an attorney I have been able to provide free legal advice to HPH, which gives me a sense of pride and allows me to repay what I can for the kindness and compassion given to me over many years.

During the first year after the girls' deaths, I attended a weekly woman's grief support group, Fresh Start, that literally saved my life. The tremendous pain of losing my first daughter and first granddaughter was more than I could emotionally and physically bear. These ladies, who had experienced their own losses (not only of children), gave me the strength and willingness to want to continue to live. Similarly, in January 2010, I attended the first Helping Parents Heal support group in Cave Creek, AZ, along with a few dozen other parents, most notably Elizabeth Boisson and Mark Ireland who chaired and presented at that meeting.

As a charter Board member and volunteer legal counsel for HPH, I have found that one very important lesson Shining Light Parents learn by sharing our stories is that we begin to heal ourselves best when we are helping others in their journeys. I continue to work with MADD as a presenter at their Victim Impact Panels and as a support group facilitator. In the past I have also done volunteer work for other organizations that seek to help those who are grieving the loss of their loved ones.

I know that Wendy and Haley are with me as I always feel their presence, with or without finding that much-treasured penny. There is no doubt that your children are always with you as well and that their communications can be either obvious or subtle. The love we share remains forever.

-Written by Wendy's Shining Light Mom and Haley's Shining Light Grandmommy, Helping Parents Heal Board Member, Founding Member and Volunteer Legal Counsel, Doryce Norwood

Shayna Elayne Smith

Shayna Elayne Smith was born on a cold winter day, January 13, 2000. She was loved before she even arrived on the planet. As our second child, Shayna, would be little sister to Kayla, who adored her and spoke to her in utero, calling her "Baby Sist."

From the start, Shayna's life was beset by complications. A prenatal test prompted us to do an amniocentesis. We found out that she was a girl and chose the name Shayna Elayne, Shayna meaning "Beautiful" and Elayne, after my godmother, meaning "Light." She would be our last child and complete our little family in this incarnation. Brian, Tywana, Kayla, and Shayna had finally arrived on the planet.

Shayna took 13 hours of labor to be born. She pooped during the delivery, complicating matters. Her heart rate kept decelerating. I was about to scream at the doctors, "Just do a C-section!" when she finally chose to arrive.

From her first hours, we knew Shayna would be a handful. The nurses on duty that night told us they had never heard a baby cry with such demand in her voice. When she wanted something, she let you know. She could and would wail for hours if necessary to get her way. In addition to being determined, she was skilled with her hands and blessed with a sharp wit and intellect. She spoke and walked early. I recall one day entering the "toy room" to find a two-year-old Shayna staring up at a gigantic Lego tower she had built herself. She was on her knees, and it towered over her head. I thought to myself, "I hope she uses her powers for good, not for evil." Thank goodness that prayer was answered.

Shayna was three years younger than her older sister, Kayla, but they were soulmates and closer than many twins. Shayna looked up to Kayla. And Kayla felt responsible for Shayna. When Shayna was about three years old, she began sleeping in Kayla's bed on several occasions. They called them "sister sleepovers." I assumed this magical time would ultimately end when Kayla kicked her out, and that Shayna would be heartbroken. I was wrong. It was Shayna who decided it was time to go back to her room. And the sister sleepovers ended with a whimper instead of a bang.

Shayna was a loving child. But she had a tongue that could cut as quickly as it built you up. So, when she started a sentence with "No offense, but...", it was time to take cover. I did most of the cooking and could usually expect a nightly rating of my accomplishments. Her highest compliment was, "This meal is restaurant-worthy."

We homeschooled both girls through the eighth grade, so for most of their early life, they attended school together. Both took to learning like ducks to water. It was as if one day, we were teaching the alphabet and the next day they could read. Shayna did her best to keep up with Kayla academically, using her big sissy as a role model.

We made it a priority to have dinner together every night if possible. When the girls were about four and seven they had a conversation at the dinner table that indicated they knew about pre-life planning, a topic we had never discussed. I'm not even sure I was aware it was a thing. They spoke about being in heaven and seeing us and choosing us as their parents. Shayna was always a deep thinker. One night she commented that she didn't fear death. She couldn't have been more than ten years old.

Shayna loved pets and wanted to be a veterinarian when she grew up. Our dog Chloe was nine years older than Shayna and we got Zoe when Shayna was about five. A year before Shayna passed, we got our third dog, Stevie. Shayna also had a pet rabbit, a gecko that passed prematurely, and a second gecko, in addition to a pair of guinea pigs. She was obsessed with birds even though she never had one as a pet. She truly adored penguins and would draw them everywhere. Pablo the Penguin was her mascot. Pee-Kwee was her

Care Bear penguin that she slept with every night. She had a penguin bedspread and slept with a penguin pillow pet. She wanted to see the penguins at the zoo and the aquarium. Her first and only job was as a volunteer at the zoo. She was only 14. She loved it.

Shayna started playing basketball at the age of five. For part of one season, she played with kids in her grade. Then she told Tywana, her coach, that she no longer wanted to play with "the babies". She moved up a grade in basketball and stayed a year ahead of her peers until at fourteen she decided her basketball career was over.

Shayna was always a favorite with her coaches. In addition to her size (she played forward or center) and her natural athleticism, she was a hard worker and a great listener. The girls were told that if they were on the left side of the basket, they should make a left-handed layup. Most, if they could, would switch to their favorite hand. Shayna never did. She was the best rebounder on the team and a tenacious defender. She would take a charge like a pro (and had two concussions to show for it).

When she reached the eighth grade, Shayna, like her sister, said she wanted to attend public school. She knew several girls at the local school through Girl Scouts. But she had never attended public school. We told her eighth grade was a tough year to make the transition. We worried that a new girl in eighth grade, particularly a Black girl in a predominantly white school district, would not be accepted.

The following year, she again expressed her desire to switch to the public schools. But the girls she had been in Scouts with were only entering eighth grade. Even though Shayna was academically advanced enough for high school work, she chose to enter eighth grade in order to be with her friends, though she took mostly ninth-grade classes. By the end of what would be her first and final year of high school, Shayna was ranked sixteenth in her class of six hundred. She was best friends with a group of six girls, all highly accomplished students. Number fifteen in the class was part of that group, and Shayna would tell her she was coming for her place.

When Shayna was 14, she decided she was done with basketball and wanted to switch to volleyball. This was a major disappointment to her high school coach, who had had his eye on Shayna since her third grade. She was to be the next center on the high school team and had been working with the current center as an apprentice. At between 5'10 and 5'11" she was still growing.

We told Shayna this would be another difficult transition. She had never played competitive volleyball. The high school season began in just three months. But we entered her in a volleyball camp over the summer. She loved it. When fall tryouts came around, she tried out for the freshman team and made it. She would go on to start on the freshman team.

When AAU volleyball started after the high school season was over, Shayna wanted to try out for that as well. Again, we tried to let her down gently. AAU is more competitive than high school, with two levels, regional and national, and she had only begun her volleyball career. When she called from the tryouts, we expected, at best, to hear she had made the regional team. However, she had been offered a spot on the national team (which cost much more and involved out-of-town travel to every game). We said yes, of course. It would turn out to be her last sports adventure. The national tournament that she played in ended three days before she transitioned from this life.

Shayna wanted to attend my alma mater, Ohio State. I was so looking forward to sharing that legacy with her. While Kayla was born in Lexington, KY, Shayna was my Buckeye Baby, born in Cincinnati, OH.

Medically, Shayna's last few years were challenging. When she was on the fifth grade AAU basketball team, she began complaining about pain in her fingers. We thought she must be jamming them in practice. She was having trouble shooting the basketball. Then the pain moved to her wrists, and we would have to wrap them before games. She adjusted and played through the pain. When we took her to the doctor, we found out she had a severe case of juvenile rheumatoid arthritis. We were devastated.

Shortly after her diagnosis, as we were headed to the lab for the confirming bloodwork, she remarked, "I wonder what it's like to get your blood taken?" She faced every challenge with a sense of adventure. She always said she wanted to break a leg so she could experience walking on crutches. Be careful what you wish for. She'd have that wish fulfilled.

She began seeing an occupational therapist. I had to give her two different drugs to combat the inflammation. One was in the form of seven pills that she had to take several hours before eating; I had to wake her up early to take them before breakfast.

The other medication was a painful injection she had to take on a weekly basis. The doctor suggested icing Shayna's arm before giving it to her in order to numb the pain. Giving her the injection would bring us both to tears, but she never complained. She never let those tears fall.

One day she asked me if we could try the injection without the ice, which took several minutes to get her arm numb. I said, "Sure, we can try it." She flinched when I gave her the shot. But, from that day on, she took the shot straight, with no ice. Shayna was my warrior.

In sixth grade, at the AAU tournament, Shayna was undercut by a girl while going for a rebound. She crumpled to the ground, grabbing her knee. Instantly, my parental instincts kicked in. I ran onto the court and scooped up that 5'8" girl and carried her off. For the remainder of the tournament, she was sidelined. I carried her around for the rest of our time there. When we took her to the doctor back home, they thought it was a torn ACL, but they weren't certain. For three weeks she was in a walking cast. When she went down in her next game, the torn ACL diagnosis was confirmed. She had surgery and got her wish to walk on crutches.

After the diagnosis of arthritis and the ACL tear, the next challenge Shayna faced was a heart condition. Every once in a while, her heart would race for a few seconds, and one day, while she was standing at the top of our stairs, she nearly passed out..

The cardiologist diagnosed her with Wolff Parkinson White syndrome. This condition is due to an extra electrical pathway in the heart. Shayna's case was mild and didn't even require medication. The doctor gave us the choice of either monitoring it or taking the aggressive approach to have surgery and correct it once and for all. This was not an easy decision. Our perfectly healthy girl had gone from no surgeries ever to surgery for injections in her fingers for arthritis, an ACL repair, and now possibly heart surgery. But we wanted to put this problem behind us. We wanted Shayna back to full health.

The procedure didn't work. We scheduled a second attempt, which was successful. The circuit disappeared, but only for a few minutes before it returned. The doctor did not recommend a third try. Shayna's condition was mild and would require nothing more than a follow-up every two years. While she was under the anesthetic, her surgeons intentionally pushed her heart into overdrive to see whether it would destabilize or settle back to normal. It always returned to normal on its own. For thirty days after the operation, Shayna wore a monitor to see whether we could catch an episode and get further detail about her condition. We rested with the idea we had done all we could, and she was fine.

On June 20, 2015, Shayna and Tywana returned from the AAU National Volleyball tournament. Shayna had had a fantastic time at the resort. Kayla and I had stayed behind to save on expenses; Shayna's volleyball season had cost us more than Kayla's first year of college. During the tournament, Tywana encouraged Shayna to call home to see how we were doing. But Shayna was having the time of her life with her friends, running the hotel halls, ordering $5 smoothies at the pool, driving around the resort in golf carts, and talking Tywana into expensive meals and desserts every night. Her attitude was, "I'll see you when I see you. I'm having a good time." This is how I believe she thinks of us now, while she's in paradise and we're still here laboring.

The Saturday Shayna returned home, Kayla left for vacation with her friends. I dropped Kayla off. I picked up Tywana and Shayna at the airport. On Monday night, Shayna had a sleepover with her friend Caroline. Tuesday, she was back in her bed, under my roof, and I felt I could sleep easy.

On June 24, I went for my usual morning walk and then headed to my home office. It was summer break, and since Shayna didn't have a job, she was supposed to help with the family business. When she didn't appear, Tywana texted her from the basement. She got no response. It wasn't unlike Shayna to be late for work. Finally, Tywana went up to get her up. That's when I heard the scream. Shayna was completely unresponsive. I performed CPR on her while Tywana called 911. It took forever for them to arrive.
At the hospital, they worked for some time on Shayna, trying to bring her around. When the chaplain entered the room where we were waiting with friends who had come to support us, we knew Shayna was gone. Or not.

For years before Shayna was born, I was afraid of death. This fear started around the time I was the age Shayna was at the time of her transition. It was a fear greater than normal; I'd call it a phobia.

Thanatophobia is the technical term for it. About five years before Shayna was born, this fear became so pressing that I started studying everything I could about death and the Afterlife in hopes of assuaging it. I learned that death is a natural transition from one stage of life to the next. It's not the end. It's a new beginning.

Because I had absorbed this at a deep level, I was fortunate to never have to worry about where Shayna was after she left life on Earth. I knew she was still alive, in better circumstances than ever before. What I did not know at the time was that "the dead" are still very much with us. They are still involved in our lives. Shayna's transition would send my search for truth into hyperdrive. I had to learn how to connect with her, to continue our relationship, until my transition, when I would join her again.

I delved deeply into podcasts and read books by mediums and other Afterlife experts about continuing our relationship with those who had passed on. A series of synchronicities led me to Mark Ireland and Elizabeth Boisson and Helping Parents Heal. About a year after Shayna passed, Tywana and I had "coincidentally" scheduled a vacation in Phoenix, AZ, where Elizabeth Boisson lives. We met Elizabeth and Ernie and Kristine Jackson and decided to start a Helping Parents Heal affiliate group in Cincinnati, OH. After a year, we and a few other parents decided to ramp up the online group of Helping Parents Heal and conduct regular web-based meetings to help other parents.

I learned to look for signs from Shayna. I thought of the conversation the girls had had years earlier about choosing us as their parents. I recalled Shayna saying she wasn't afraid to die. While making her final arrangements, we were torn between burial versus cremation for our daughter. Tywana and I discussed it and decided on cremation. We did not want our memories of Shayna to be tied to a location. When we ran our decision by Kayla to get her thoughts, she told us this story.

On Mother's Day 2015, about six weeks before Shayna's transition, we were at my brother's house. Shayna was outside with her cousins and Kayla. No one was talking about death. The group ranged in age from 15 to 19. Shayna mentioned that when she died, she wanted to be cremated and have her ashes spread under a tree. This settled the matter for us. We had her cremated, and her ashes are scattered under a tree in our front yard today.

Shayna has sent us signs too numerous to put into this short chapter. I have had many medium readings, during which Shayna comes through loud and clear with incredible evidence. Some of the most impressive have been with Suzanne Giesemann, with whom Shayna has a special connection. During one reading, Suzanne accurately described the "happy thought bubble," a purple glass orb, similar to a Christmas ornament, that hangs in our kitchen. Shayna also frequently "drops in" on Suzanne with messages and further evidence.

After Suzanne had conveyed the information about the happy thought bubble, she called to ask if the bubble was cracked at the top. Neither of us had noticed such a crack, so I took it down and examined it. Along the top I found a barely visible hairline crack. Suzanne then delivered the message that Shayna had noticed it before we did! During another call, Suzanne told Tywana that Shayna had mentioned some mala beads a friend had given her mother, along with a book on using them, and that Tywana had a question about them. After some thought, Tywana nodded. While meditating with the beads, she would often feel her heart quicken and see the color purple. Her question was, "Is this Shayna?" Shayna confirmed that it was.

During another call, Suzanne had a message to deliver, but wanted to provide some evidence first. She asked if Shayna's sister Kayla had been playing basketball recently. This time we knew Suzanne was wrong; Kayla hates playing sports other than swimming. But we had to call her to check. When we asked if she had been playing basketball, predictably, she said no. However, she was babysitting two young girls that summer, and the day before, they had been using Play-Doh to make little balls and pretend they were basketballs.

On Shayna's fifth angelversary date, I was hoping for a sign but careful not to get my hopes up. I was zoned out driving Tywana to a doctor's appointment when she pointed to the truck stopped ahead of us at a light. A sticker on the tailgate announced in huge letters, "I'm right here." On the truck's back window another sticker indicated the truck's origin, the word "Home" with the O replaced by the outline of the home state. The state was Ohio, our home, and Shayna's birthplace. The message was clear.

Between conducting Helping Parents Heal meetings and talking to thousands of parents over the years, I have found healing and meaning in my new life. Four years after Shayna's transition, I began my ministry of sorts, called Grief 2 Growth.

Drawing on my studies and my years of experience with HPH, I composed a handbook on handling grief. Next, I started a life-coaching business specializing in helping people transform their grief into growth. Finally, I launched a podcast, and as of August 2021, I have recorded my 150th episode.

I would not be doing what I am doing today had it not been for the presence of Shayna in my life and the knowledge I have gained from her transition into her next life. Shayna, my beautiful light, is the inspiration for all I do. She is the lighthouse that is guiding me Home.

-Written by Shayna's Shining Light Dad, Helping Parents Heal Board Member, Presenter and Caring Listener, Brian Smith

How to Heal from the Passing of a Child

1-Know that your child is not gone. The veil that separates you from your son or daughter is as thin as a sheet of wax paper. And when we see them again, we will feel as though not one second has passed. As Suzanne Giesemann so eloquently puts it, our kids are *Still Right Here*.

2-Take one breath at a time, then one minute at a time, until you are ready to move forward. Everyone's journey is different. Don't compare yours to anyone else's. You are unique, just as your child is unique.

3-Know that your child is happy, healthy, and 'home' and we are still 'in school.' [1] And we have so much to accomplish before we hug our kids again! But for now, they walk beside us, holding our hands and leading the way to healing.

4-Surround yourself with friends who understand. Our kids in spirit are all friends with each other; it is they who have connected us here on Earth. Expand your friend base to include those who love to hear about your child in spirit. We keep them alive in our hearts and spirits by continuing to tell their stories.

5-Be Kind, both to yourself and others. Helping others helps us even more. Once you move forward on the path to healing, reach a hand back to help others who are not so far along the path.

6-Express Gratitude. We have so much to be grateful for on this journey. Watch for the signs and gifts that your children send you and be sure to always thank them. This will automatically bring more gifts!

[1] Mark Ireland's beautiful wife Susie explained this to me early on in my journey to healing.

7-Express Forgiveness, for yourself and others. We cannot heal without letting go of the feelings of guilt and anger that hold us back.

8-Live each day in honor of your child in spirit. They are so proud of us, and they share in everything we do.

9-Raise your vibration. Eat healthy, plant-based foods, practice yoga and meditation, take long hikes outdoors, take off your shoes and connect your feet to the earth, use crystals and essential oils, use sound meditation and breathing exercises and again, practice kindness wherever you go.

10-Learn to communicate with your child in spirit, through automatic writing, guided meditation, the pendulum, dream visits, mirror gazing, forest bathing, reiki and much more. We can all do this! And our kids high-five each other when they see us smile.

~ Elizabeth Boisson

Resources

Many of the Shining Light Parents included in this book have written their own helpful, healing books. Others have created nonprofits in honor of their children. Craig McMahon has produced healing documentaries. Please be sure to check out these wonderful resources:

Our Books

Tyler Lives, Mom, I'm Not Gone by Carol Sanna Allen

SHIFT: The Spiritual Awakening of a Grieving Father by Jason Durham

Messages of Hope, Wolf's Messages, Still Right Here, In The Silence, Love Beyond Words,

and *Droplets of God* by Suzanne Giesemann

The Medium Next Door by Maureen Hancock

How to Live When You Want to Die by LeAnn Hull

Soul Shift, Finding Where the Dead Go by Mark Ireland

Quinton's Messages, Quinton's Legacy by Ernie Jackson

The Myth of Dying by Linda McCarthy

Knowing by Jeffery Olsen

Where are You? by Jeffery and Spencer Olsen

The Ripple Effect - Invisible Impact of Suicide by Laurie Savoie

Grief 2 Growth, Planted, Not Buried by Brian Smith

Soul Smart by Susanne Wilson

Nonprofits

Helping Parents Heal - www.helpingparentsheal.org

The Andy Hull Sunshine Foundation - www.andyssunshine.com

Carly's Kids - www.carlyskidsfoundation.com

The Healing Cross Project - www.healingcrossproject.com

Documentaries

The Life to Afterlife Spirituality Series by Craig McMahon
~Mom, Can You Hear Me?
~I Died, Now What?
~Death and Back 1, 2 and 3
~Tragedy By Design
~I Want to Talk to the Dead
~The Healers

More About Helping Parents Heal

Our Mission: Helping Parents Heal is a non-profit organization dedicated to assisting bereaved parents to become Shining Light Parents by providing support and resources to aid in the healing process. We go a step beyond other groups by allowing the open discussion of spiritual experiences and evidence for the afterlife, in a non-dogmatic way. Affiliate groups welcome everyone regardless of religious (or non-religious) background and allow for open dialog.

A Special Thanks to our Editor, Shining Light Mom of Kiara, Zoe English Kharpertian

Kiara was and remains the light and inspiration of our lives, and of so many others. During her brave fight with metastatic breast cancer, a fight that lasted nearly six years, she completed her Ph.D., mentored dozens of students, got married, pursued her passions of horseback riding and rock climbing, and enriched the lives of countless family, friends and acquaintances with her warmth, kindness, and brilliance. Her blog can be found at: https://wordsfromwardfour.wordpress.com , where her spirit and comfort to others endures. She was a gift, and gave us 31 golden years, for which we are eternally grateful.

-Written by Kiara's Shining Light Mom, Zoe English Kharpertian

Gratitude

Many wonderful people have endeavored to make this book a reality. First and foremost, I am grateful to Morgan, to Chelsea, and to all of our kids who have worked overtime to publish this book. It has come together in less than two months. Thank you, Jamie Clark, for delivering Morgan's message that this book needed to be written.

I am grateful to the parents who are part of this book for sharing their exceptional children with you and me. Their stories are part of my healing journey. It is heartwarming that Craig McMahon understood that our kids are *not gone*, and that this message needed to reach a broader audience. And thank you, Zoe English Kharpertian and Laurie Savoie, for tirelessly editing the book.

Our nonprofit is 100% volunteer, and the goal of everyone who is a part of it is to help others heal. I am grateful to our HPH Affiliate Leaders, Caring Listeners, Board Members, and Presenters, who give freely of their time and energy to parents and families throughout the world, every day. I am especially grateful to Irene Vouvalides, with whom I speak multiple times a day. And to Carol Allen, who immediately began helping others after the passing of her son Tyler.

I am grateful to Suzanne Giesemann and Maureen Hancock for being a part of HPH and writing beautiful forewords for this book.

And above all, I am grateful to my family; my husband Cyril, and my daughters, Alix and Christine; who have supported me and HPH throughout this healing journey and have allowed their stories to be told.

If you would like to donate to Helping Parents Heal, please purchase a copy of this book. 100% of the proceeds go to helping parents and families heal. You can also do so online at: www.helpingparentsheal.org.

And thank you for reading this book and for supporting our work at Helping Parents Heal. Please help us spread the word far and wide that our kids are *still right here!!*

-Elizabeth Boisson

Our Contributors

Our Contributors in Alphabetical Order: *Carol Allen, Elizabeth Boisson, Kim Camacho, Kim Courtney, Jason Durham, Glenn and Nita Erickson, Suzanne and Ty Giesemann, Jeff and Lynn Hollahan, LeAnn Hull, Mark Ireland, Kristine and Ernie Jackson, Zoe English Kharpertian, Linda McCarthy, Craig McMahon, Doryce Norwood, Jeffery Olsen, Laurie Savoie, Brian and Tywana Smith, Irene Vouvalides, and Michelle Ziff.*

Printed in Great Britain
by Amazon